台北

台北

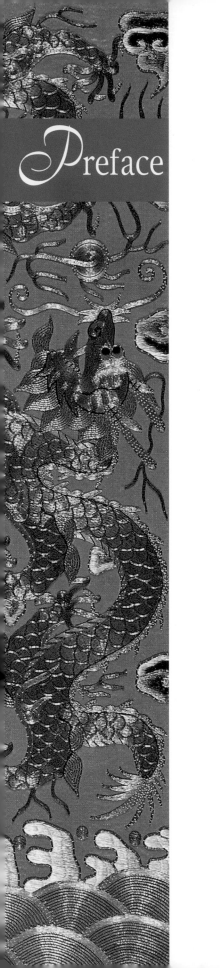

Preface

Preface

The National Palace Museum, located on the outskirts of Taipei in the suburb of Wai-shuang-hsi, is one of the largest museums in the world. Renowned for its unique and extensive collection, the Museum is a prime destination for foreign visitors. Unfortunately, despite its distinguished reputation, few of the local Taiwanese populace regularly frequent or enjoy the splendors it has to offer. As one whose success depends largely on the popularity of the Museum, I dare not take this issue lightly. Thus, my colleagues and I have given much thought as to the best way to present the Museum and its beautiful collection, while encouraging diversity among our patrons.

The visitor is a guest, and as a host, the Museum must accommodate the individual needs of each guest in order to ensure an experience unlike any other. We cannot lecture a child as we would an academician, and vice versa. Oftentimes, silence is the most effective method for education, as the works of art speak for themselves.

Recently, we have taken various measures to further our outreach programs, and I would like to thank all those involved, in particular those who assisted with the English audio guides. This book is part of our ongoing effort to meld art and life. A good guidebook is the key to art appreciation. It is our hope that with this guide, the art on the walls of the National Palace Museum, and in your daily life, will no longer seem distant and insignificant.

Tu Cheng-sheng
Director of the National Palace Museum

Contents

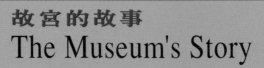

故宫的故事
The Museum's Story

❶ Founding of the Museum

The Museum traces its roots to the Nationalist Revolution that overthrew the Ch'ing monarchy. This eventually led to the formal departure of the last emperor, P'u I, from the Forbidden City in 1924.

❷ Forming of the Committee for the Preservation of the Ch'ing Palace

The Committee entered the Palace and itemized the inner court collection, which led to the formal founding of the National Palace Museum on October 10, 1925.

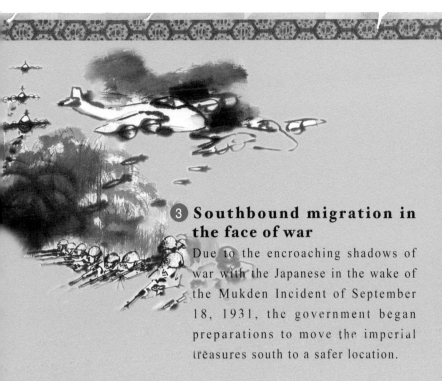

3 Southbound migration in the face of war

Due to the encroaching shadows of war with the Japanese in the wake of the Mukden Incident of September 18, 1931, the government began preparations to move the imperial treasures south to a safer location.

4 Further migration due to war

In 1933, the government evacuated the collection to Shanghai, where it remained until the 1936 completion of special storage facilities in the Nationalist capital of Nanking. However, in 1937, the Marco Polo Bridge Incident forced government officials to evacuate the treasures once again, this time to the western provinces of Kweichow and Szechwan.

⑤ Naval transports arrive in Keelung

After the victory over the Japanese in 1945, the government ordered the return of the collection to Nanking. However, ongoing political instability soon forced the Nationalist government to move the collection via ship to the port of Keelung on the island of Taiwan.

⑥ Wu-feng, Taichung

From 1950 to 1965, the collection was temporarily stored at a site called Pei-kou in Wu-feng, Taichung.

❼ Permanent home in Wai-shuang-hsi, Taipei

With the completion of the present facilities, the imperial treasures finally found their permanent resting place. Over the past fifty years, the Museum's holdings, which comprise the collections of both the Ch'ing court and the National Central Museum of Nanking, have increased through donations and purchases to the present monumental scope of over 650,000 items.

The Museum and Its History

Recent years have seen the founding of many public and private museums in Taiwan. Amongst these various institutions, the National Palace Museum has consistently assumed the heavy responsibility of protecting the treasures of China's past and glorifying Chinese culture. The Museum's worldwide reputation and international status rest on the beauty and refinement of its priceless collection.

Founding of the Museum

The National Palace Museum traces its earliest roots to the Nationalist Revolution that overthrew the Ch'ing monarchy and ultimately led to the

formal departure of P'u I, the last emperor, from the Forbidden City in 1924. This resulted in the creation of the Committee for the Preservation of the Ch'ing Palace, which entered the court to itemize the collection and, on October 10, 1925, formally founded the National Palace Museum.

Early curators cataloging the Ch'ing palace collection.

Years of Hardship

As the threat of war with Japan increased in the wake of the Mukden Incident of September 18, 1931, the government grew increasingly concerned for the safety of the imperial treasures. This concern led to a decision to move the collection to safer facilities in the South, a process that began in February 1933, with the evacuation of the treasures to Shanghai. The completion of special storage facilities in Nanking in

August 1936 provided a new home for the collection, which was relocated from Shanghai in December of that year. The Marco Polo Bridge Incident of 1937, which ignited the Sino-Japanese war, forced the evacuation of the collection once again, this time in three separate groups to different locations in the western Chinese provinces of Kweichow and Szechwan.

After defeating the Japanese in 1945, the government ordered the return of the collection to Nanking. However, ongoing instability soon led the Nationalist government to move it yet again, this time via ship from Shanghai to the port of Keelung on Taiwan. It was only in 1950 that the collection reached Wu-feng, Taichung, where it was temporarily stored at a site known as Pei-kou. With the 1965 completion of the present National Palace Museum in Wai-shuang-hsi on the outskirts of Taipei, these precious treasures, priceless heirlooms of both the Chinese and global community, finally found a sanctuary and ended their years of wandering.

Above: The collection's temporary home in Wu-feng, Taichung.
Below: Moving the collection.

Process of Construction

When first completed in 1965, the Museum's facilities were limited to the central portion of the present main exhibition building. In order to expand the exhibition space and develop a better environment for both visitors and the collection, the Museum has, over the intervening decades, undergone four phases of expansion. These renovations included the construction of the east and west wings, the east and west rooftop pavilions, the Chih-shan and Chih-te gardens, and the library building.

While the yellow wall tiling and green roof tiles that adorn the Museum evoke traditional Chinese architecture, great energy was expended to ensure that, within this classical superstructure, visitors could experience the sophisticated and spacious atmosphere of a modern museum.

In the beginning, the Museum facilities were limited to the central hall of the current Main Building.

The Collection and Its Contents

The National Palace Museum inherited the art collection of the Ch'ing court, itself the culmination of a millennium of imperial collecting by the emperors and royal families of the Sung (960-1279), Yüan (1279-

1368), Ming (1368-1644), and Ch'ing (1644-1911) dynasties. All told, this abundant treasure trove now numbers some 650,000 items, divided into three categories: antiquities, painting and calligraphy, and rare books and documents.

The antiquities collection contains over 70,000 bronzes, ceramics, jades, pieces of lacquer and enamelware, carvings, and other precious artifacts. Of these, the Museum's collection of Chinese ceramics, which includes particularly rare examples of Sung dynasty Ju, Kuan, and other wares, is ranked both in number and quality as the foremost collection of ceramics worldwide.

The painting and calligraphy collection, which also includes rubbings and textiles, numbers over 10,000 items, and features famous works of every major artist from the sixth century A.D. to the end of the imperial era. The Museum's collection of Sung dynasty painting is particularly noteworthy, including classic works such as *Travelers Among Mountains and Streams*, *Early Spring*, and *Wind in Pines Among Myriad Valleys*.

The rare books and documents collection features rare printed editions, written works in Mongolian and Manchu, and a wide variety of archival records, which combined total over 570,000 volumes and individual documents. This includes the only surviving examples of certain rare books, original records of major historical events, and other priceless texts.

The precious treasures are displayed for the public in long-term survey exhibitions and short-term special exhibits focused on specific topics. In addition to exhibitions held in the main building, the Museum library to the left of the central concourse provides an excellent variety of art and historically-related materials for Museum staff and public use.

Suggestions and Guidelines for Visiting the Museum

* Bring a backpack to hold such necessities as a water bottle, camera, and notebook, as well as the souvenirs and informational materials you collect during your visit.

* Wear loose, comfortable clothing, preferably with pockets for tickets, pen, and paper.

* Museum galleries are climate-controlled to help preserve the collection. We recommend that visitors bring an extra layer of clothing.

* It is best to wear comfortable, casual shoes to lighten the burden on your feet. The Museum is very large, and a thorough visit requires a lot of walking and long periods of standing in one place. Wearing hard, leather shoes can quickly lead to tired, sore feet.

* Bring a notebook to record and sketch your observations. It is a good opportunity to enhance your experience and commemorate your visit.

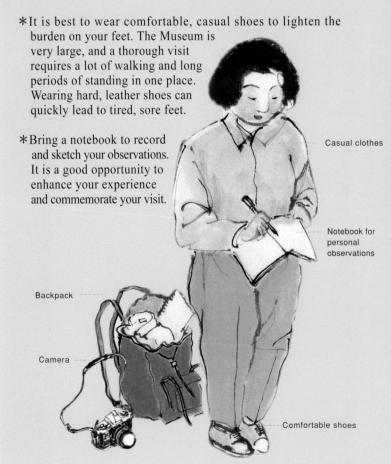

Casual clothes

Notebook for personal observations

Backpack

Camera

Comfortable shoes

Museum Regulations

* Visitors are requested to dress neatly and are discouraged from wearing slip-on sandals in the Museum.

* Please do not bring pets, food, or beverages into the Museum.

* Smoking, gum, and betel nut prohibited.

* Boisterous activity, running, and littering prohibited.

* While photography is allowed in some galleries, the use of flashes or tripods is not permitted. All photography is expressly prohibited in the painting and calligraphy galleries.

Helpful Hints

* A wealth of information is available on the Museum website. Be sure to take advantage of this excellent resource prior to your visit by logging on at http://www.npm.gov.tw.

* Please confirm gallery, special exhibit, and activity times prior to your visit.

* The Museum's regularly scheduled daily tours are great way to get an in-depth look at the collection. Remember to consult tour times and register at the information desk upon arriving.

* Please bring relevant identification when you apply for any of the special visitor programs and services offered by the Museum.

* The checkroom can store personal belongings and also provides strollers and wheelchairs for visitor use.

* After entering the museum, please keep your ticket stub so that you may leave and re-enter at will.

* In addition to visiting the exhibitions, take advantage of the many lectures, symposiums, and other educational activities organized by the Museum.

* When visiting the galleries, be sure to take advantage of the free handouts and other explanatory material. Not only are they excellent souvenirs, but also an easy way to build your own archive of information on the Museum and its collection.

The Beginning of the Journey

The National Palace Museum holds one of the largest collections of Chinese art in the world. For thousands of years, through labor and innovation, Chinese craftsmen and artisans created beautiful works of jade, ceramic, bronze, painting, calligraphy, and other media. Yet these works were more than just "art," they were instrumental in helping to build and define a civilization—the Chinese civilization. Each work of art is a testament to the skill and talent of its creators, and the lasting impression they left upon the world.

Art and the Emperor

Most of the objects you will see in the National Palace Museum once belonged to the collections of the imperial court. Many Chinese emperors were well-versed in the literature and art of the past. The contents of their personal collections demonstrated the breadth of their knowledge and power. In a way, we owe a debt to these rulers for the pride they took in these collections and the refined taste with which they amassed artifacts. Without imperial patronage, the works would not have survived the perils of the ages, and we would not be able to admire and enjoy them today.

T'ang dynasty

Portrait of T'ai-tsung

The Enlightened Leader of the Early T'ang

Monarchs and members of the aristocracy were key patrons of the arts during the T'ang dynasty (618-907). The art produced under their support was imbued with a strong sense of political morality, with emphasis placed on styles that expressed the magnificence and splendor of the court.

T'ai-tsung (598-649), the second emperor of the T'ang, established an ideal state, famous in later eras for its enlightened administration. A skilled practitioner and connoisseur of calligraphy, T'ai-tsung particularly admired the work of the famous fourth century master calligrapher Wang Hsi-chih. His admiration for Wang's writing style forms an important chapter in the history of Chinese calligraphy, which is reflected in the painting *Hsiao I Stealing the Orchid Pavilion Preface* and in a Sung-era rubbing of the *Orchid Pavilion Preface*, both in the Museum's collection.

Portrait of T'ai-tsung, T'ang dynasty

Ode to the Wagtail

Hsüan-tsung (685-762), the sixth emperor of the T'ang dynasty, had an innate talent for the arts that led him to become a skilled musician and calligrapher. Here, we see a fine example of the emperor's semi-cursive calligraphy. The brushwork possesses a stark and powerful beauty, and conveys the imposing majesty of the T'ang imperial house.

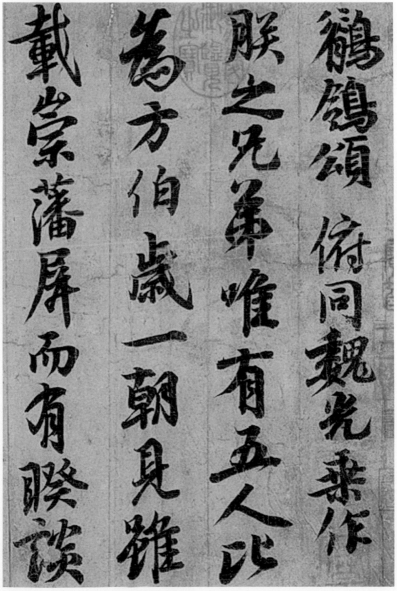

Ode to the Wagtail, Hsüan-tsung, T'ang dynasty

Portrait of Hui-tsung

Emperor and Esthete

Chao Chi (1082-1135), known to history as the Emperor Hui-tsung, was a man of abundant talents. He exerted a tremendous influence on the arts of both his own era and of the centuries to follow. Under his direction, the court collected, organized, and restored masterpieces of former dynasties, the titles of which they compiled into a catalogue known as the *Hsüan-ho hua-p'u* (*Painting Catalogue of the Hsüan-ho Era*). Hui-tsung established a painting academy, where he personally directed painters in copying important historical works and tested both their skill at depicting natural subjects and the depth of their literary training. His exams often called on painters to visually depict a given verse or phrase, such as, "Where does the bell toll in the deep mountains?" Such questions encouraged academy painters to create an imaginary space beyond the visual, an approach that had a tremendous influence on the painting of later centuries.

Hui-tsung was also an elegant master of the brush who wrote in a distinctively strong, untrammeled style. His surviving works of painting and calligraphy are masterpieces that demonstrate his achievements as an artist.

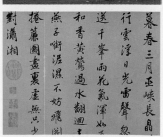

Above: Portrait of Hui-tsung, Sung dynasty
Center: Chimonanthus and Birds, Hui-tsung, Sung dynasty
Below: Poem in Seven Character Regulated Verse Kao-tsung, Sung dynasty

Sung dynasty Kao-tsung

Poem in Seven Character Regulated Verse

Chao Kou (1107-1187), known to history as the emperor Kao-tsung, was the son of Hui-tsung. After the conquest of North China by the Jurchen in 1127, Kao-tsung led the court into exile in the South, establishing what came to be known as the Southern Sung dynasty (1127-1279). An artist of substantial learning and natural talent, Kao-tsung focused much of his aesthetic energies on the art of writing.

This piece, written in standard script with an upright brush, is a copy of a poem by Tu Fu (712-770). Also known as *Verse From the Last Month of Spring*, the characters that compose the work are balanced, and the overall piece is written in a relaxed fashion that simultaneously communicates stability and liveliness. Tu Fu's poem is almost painterly in its descriptiveness, a quality that blends with the artfulness of Kao-tsung's calligraphy to improve the emotive quality of both the writing and content.

Yüan dynasty

Portrait of Shih-tsu

The Mongol Khan Who Built an Empire

Yüan Shih-tsu (1215-1294), better known in the West by his Mongolian name Khubilai Khan, was the grandson of Chinggis Khan. By conquering the Southern Sung, he reunified China, which had been divided for 150 years. The scale of the Mongol empire during the reign of Khubilai was unprecedented, with territory stretching across Asia and into Eastern Europe. An expert at selecting skilled subordinates, Khubilai adopted Confucian administrative techniques, promoted classical education and the rule of law, and thereby ruled a vast domain for three and a half decades.

Portrait of Shih-tsu, Yüan dynasty

Portrait of Hsüan-tsung

Chu Chan-chi (1399-1435), the emperor Hsüan-tsung, ruled China for ten years in an era that he proclaimed the "Reign of Propagating Moral Virtue" (Hsüan-te). By the reign of Hsüan-tsung, the emphasis early Ming emperors had placed on imperial reconstruction finally came to fruition. With a prosperous economy and relative degree of social harmony, the Hsüan-tsung era was the Ming dynasty's greatest period of political stability. Prior to ascending the throne, Hsüan-tsung served in military campaigns to the north and south of China, and thus understood and sympathized with the suffering of the common people. As a result, he focused his energies on the affairs of the state.

However, despite the depth of his involvement in administrative matters, Hsüan-tsung still found time for artistic pursuits. A man of substantial literary and calligraphic ability, he mastered the genres of landscape, figure, bird-and-flower, and insect painting. He also received training in the pursuit of arms, and is remembered as a fine ruler and warrior-poet.

Ming dynasty Hsüan-tsung

Three Auspicious Goats

This work portrays a pair of suckling baby goats whose soft and yielding fur is depicted in a highly naturalistic, lifelike manner, a departure from traditional Chinese painting. Hsüan-tsung completed the piece in 1429 at the age of thirty-one.

Above: Portrait of Hsüan-tsung, Ming dynasty
Below: Three Auspicious Goats, Hsüan-tsung, Ming dynasty

Emperor Ch'ien-lung's Imperial Seals

Ch'ien-lung (1711-1799), the fourth son of Emperor Yung-cheng, was the longest living emperor in Chinese history. From an early age, Ch'ien-lung was praised above his siblings for his exceptional skills and talents, and drew favor from his grandfather, the Emperor K'ang-hsi (1654-1722). Thus, despite Yung-cheng's implementation of a secret heir selection process, the choice of Ch'ien-lung as heir apparent was obvious to all long before his father's death.

Upon assuming the throne at the young age of twenty-five, Ch'ien-lung proved his worth. Taking inspiration from his grandfather's benevolent reign and incorporating procedures from his father's harsh and disciplined rule, the emperor solidified imperial power, pacified the bordering tribes, and led the Ch'ing dynasty into its most glorious era.

Ch'ien-lung was an avid collector of art. Most of the treasures in the National Palace Museum, including many paintings and works of calligraphy, bronze vessels, antiquities, and rare books, were once part of his collection. The scope of his acquisitions is evidenced in the variety of seals and inscriptions that he left on many of these objects.

Above: Ch'ien-lung imperial seal,
    Ch'ing dynasty
Center: Seal imprint, Ch'ing dynasty
Below: Ch'ien-lung's summer hat,
    Ch'ing dynasty

Bronze

Bronze is an alloy composed of copper, tin, and small amounts of lead. Prior to the development of iron technology, bronze was the strongest metal available and was well suited for the production of sharp weapons. The forging of bronze objects requires a high degree of technical sophistication. In Chinese civilization, this knowledge was attained in approximately 2000 B.C., which corresponds roughly to the legendary Hsia dynasty. The subsequent Shang and Chou dynasties are generally regarded as the golden age of Chinese bronze art.

The early Chinese believed that the spirits of their ancestors held the power to influence and control the natural forces of the material world. In an effort to avoid calamity and enjoy good fortune, they regularly worshipped the dead through sacrificial offerings of food. At this time, bronze was primarily used for producing vessels to hold these sacrificial offerings. Thus, as they were employed in the most important rituals of the state, bronzes became a symbol of monarchic authority. Many vessels were buried in tombs alongside the dead, and the excavation of such tombs has provided the majority of the bronzes known to date. A large number of the bronzes that survive today bear cast inscriptions which help scholars date them and interpret their function. The inscriptions also provide important information about the development of calligraphy.

Chart of Bronze Vessel Types

	Ting	Li	Yen
food vessels			

	Chüeh	Chiao	Chia
wine vessels			

	Tsun	Yu	Ho
wine vessels			

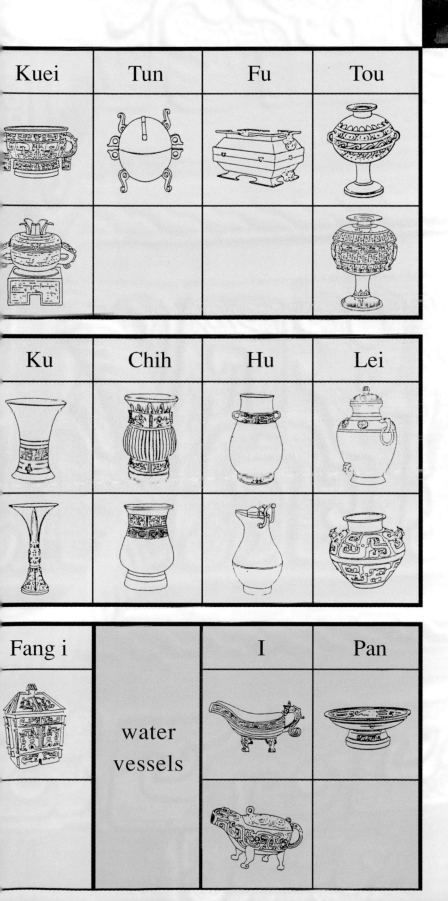

Kuei	Tun	Fu	Tou

Ku	Chih	Hu	Lei

Fang i	water vessels	I	Pan

Tsung Chou Chung

The *chung*, which is generally referred to as a bell in English, was a percussion instrument used in ancient ritual music. This particular example was used by the son-of-heaven, or ruler, of the Western Chou (1122 - 771 B.C.). During the Shang dynasty (1765-1122 B.C.), chung were generally placed "upside down," with the mouth facing up. This alignment was reversed in the Chou dynasty, which required that the instrument be hung from a beam or framework in order to be rung. The two sides of this chung are adorned with thirty-six nipple-like protrusions. Some scholars interpret these as a means of modifying the tone of the bell, while other suggests that they are simply a form of decoration.

What makes the Tsung Chou Chung particularly famous is its long inscription. Running 123 characters in length, the inscription begins on the flat central panel of the bell and continues on first the left, then the right, lower registers. The inscription records an invasion by the southern kingdom of P'u during the reign of the King Li. The Chou army, under the direct command of the king, successfully turned back the invaders. After his triumphant return to the capital, Li had the bell cast to commemorate his ancestors for their assistance in assuring his victory. The inscription also includes the characters *ts'ang-ts'ang ts'ong-ts'ong*, which describe the sound of the chiming bell and remind us that, in its original context, the chung was not merely a source of visual stimulation, but also auditory pleasure.

Tsung Chou Chung, Western Chou dynasty

San P'an

According to traditional Chinese nomenclature, the term *p'an* refers to a type of water vessel. This particular p'an bears an inscription 357 characters in length, the content of which describes a land dispute between the states of Ts'e and San. The characters are divided by faint raised lines, in a manner consistent with the style of inscriptions from the late Western Chou. Ts'e's invasion of San territory led to a long string of conflicts and skirmishes, which eventually required the intervention of the central Chou government. The Chou king dispatched the Agriculture Minister Chung Nung to investigate and resolve the matter. Under his direction, the two states performed a truce ceremony in the Tou-hsin Palace. In the course of this ceremony, the fifteen representatives of Ts'e presented the representatives of San with agricultural implements and a map redefining the political boundary between the two states. This p'an was then cast to record and seal the treaty.

The outer edge of the p'an bears three registers of so-called k'uei dragon motifs. The dragon heads rise off the surface of the vessel in high relief, while their more schematic bodies stretch out to either side. On the ringed foot at the bottom of the vessel are six animal mask motifs represented in the typical simplified fashion of the late Western Chou. Due to the length and historical value of its inscription, the San P'an has been a focal point of scholarly attention since its excavation in the Ch'ing dynasty.

Above: San P'an, Late Westren Chou dynasty
Right: Tsu-i Tsun, Early Western Chou dynasty

Tsu-i Tsun

The *tsun* is a type of Shang and Chou dynasty ritual water vessel. This magnificently crafted tsun has a unique shape, and includes an inscription on its inner surface. The inscription reads "Tsun made for Grandfather I." The body of the vessel is decorated with vertical flanges, with buffalo mask-like motifs integrated into the designs on front and back. The features of this exquisitely crafted tsun possess a lifelike quality, and the piece stands as testimony to the mastery of ancient bronze casters.

Mao-kung Ting

The *ting*, or tripod vessel, served as an ancient cooking pot. During the Shang and Chou dynasties, the ting came to symbolize power and authority, and served as the most important vessel in ritual offering ceremonies.

The Mao-kung Ting is a classic example of late Western Chou bronze. Very few decorations adorn the vessel body, and it lacks the typical mysterious and flamboyant animal mask décor, possessing only a simple ring-like motif. However, the historical significance of the Mao-kung vessel lies not in its décor, but rather in the inscription found on its interior. The inscription primarily contains words of praise from the King of Chou for the Duke of Mao. The Duke of Mao, who assisted the king with various affairs of state, was a responsible public servant highly regarded in his lifetime. The production of this ting, therefore, provides words of encouragement and guidance for the Duke's descendants, in the hope that they too will live similarly exemplary lives. The Mao-kung Ting, with its sturdy and mas-sive form and uniquely molded animal-hoofed legs, was often copied, on a smaller scale, in later periods.

Mao-kung Ting, Late Western Chou dynasty

The Ting and Political Authority

There is a traditional Chinese belief that regards the ting as a symbol of monarchic power and authority. Legend holds that King Yü of the Hsia dynasty cast nine ting as symbols of the nine prefectures under his control. Other early stories allege that only those with the ability to become emperor had the wherewithal to create ting. Thus, those seeking political power often cast ting as a means of legitimating their own imperial ambitions. While the truth of these legends is open to speculation, the vessels are clearly potent expressions of strength and severity. Over time, their original purpose was overshadowed by a new role as one of the primary implements used in official state ritual. Reserved exclusively for the use of the ruler and upper classes, they naturally developed associations with political power and authority.

The Animal Mask Motif

Many ancient Chinese bronzes are decorated with a mask-like animal face design. These designs predominate on bronzes dating from the early Shang (sixteenth to fourteenth century B.C.) to the beginnings of the Chou dynasty (eleventh to tenth century B.C.), after which they were gradually replaced by other motifs.

What sort of animal does the mask represent? There are several theories. Scholars have identified some thirty different types of masks that include, among others, the visual characteristics of bulls, tigers, elephants, deer, and birds. These animals, filtered through human imagination, are transformed on bronze into visages of awe and mystery. The focal element of each mask is its pair of staring eyes; other elements, such as the nose, eyebrows, and ears, tend to be simple and schematic. Some masks are further enhanced by the addition of horns, claws, and fangs.

Hsi-tsun with turquoise, malachite, and gold inlay

Tsun is often used as a general term for bronze ritual vessels, while *hsi-tsun* refers specifically to animal-shaped vessels. During the Warring States period (453-221 B.C.), bronze casters frequently adorned their creations with turquoise inlay.

There are only a few known examples of animal-shaped wine vessels that can be attributed to state ancestral temples of the Warring States era, which makes this fine, heavy-bodied tsun particularly rare. Judging from its stocky profile and hoofs, the vessel appears to represent a water buffalo. However, the absence of horns and the raised, long, and sharply pointed ears may also suggest a rhinoceros whose nose horn has been cut away. According to recent archeological evidence, rhinoceroses inhabited the middle and lower reaches of the Yellow River during the Shang and Chou dynasties.

The vessel, measuring 28.5 centimeters in height and weighing 5.21 kilograms, bears a removable lid on its back and a spout at its mouth. The thick neck is decorated with a gilded band and the area around its eyes is inlaid with turquoise. The entire vessel is further adorned with diagonal *lei wen* (thunder patterns) and gold and silver inlay, giving it a spirited quality that is at once detailed, natural, and unassuming.

Hsi-tsun with turquoise, malachite, and gold inlay, Middle Warring States period

Chia-liang Measure

Ancient bronze vessels were traditionally used during ritual ceremonies and burials, yet this bronze measure was created for an entirely different purpose. Following Wang Mang's successful coup against the reigning Han dynasty, the new ruler changed the dynasty name to Hsin (A.D.9-25), and, among other new policies, sought to establish a unified system of weights and measures. To this end, he ordered the fashioning of this and other bronze measures. These new measures provided a volume standard for grain and wheat containers throughout the country. The measures were intentionally casted from bronze, which, as a symbol of endurance and longevity, symbolized the dream of an eternal standard.

The measure contains an inscription 216 words in length, written in the standard seal script of the Han dynasty. The inscription records the origins of the measure, the various ways it was put to use, and the basic units of measurement. According to the engraving, the numerical value that the Chinese found for *pi* was 3.1457, very close to the modern estimation of 3.1416. The precision of the measurement demonstrates the early advancement of Chinese scientific knowledge.

Chia-liang Measure, Wang Mang Interregnum, Hsin dynasty

Oracle Bones

During the nineteenth century, the inhabitants of the district of Anyang, located in Honan province, began regularly unearthing broken pieces of turtle shell and cattle bone near the village of Hsiao-t'un. They sold these pieces to local apothecaries, who subsequently ground them up to use as a medicinal ingredient. In 1899, a Chinese scholar inadvertently discovered that many of these bones bore mysterious inscribed symbols. The discovery captured the attention of the scholarly community, who soon determined that the inscriptions were important records of Shang dynasty divinatory rituals. After a century of research, we now recognize that the inscriptions are written in the earliest known systematic form of Chinese writing, and that their content deals with both the daily life of the Shang king and the affairs of the Shang state. Thus, the inscriptions not only act as precious sources of information for the study of the development of Chinese script, but also provide a direct record of China's ancient history.

China's Earliest Fortunetelling?

The people who inhabited northern China some three thousand ago were intensely curious about the mysteries of nature. Unable to explain the forces that created rain, thunder, and lightning, nor understand the human cycles of birth and death, they looked to their deities, and the spirits of their ancestors, for guidance. The king sought guidance through the help of a royal diviner, who one might call the forefather of Chinese fortunetellers. Yet this diviner did not read palms or chart the signs of the zodiac, but rather used turtle shells and cattle bones to consult the spirit world.

The Divination Process

The inscribed divinatory bones of the Shang dynasty are derived from two primary sources—turtle plastrons (underbelly shells) and cattle scapula. Prior to divination, the bones were cleaned, washed, and pared flat. Several small depressions were then bored in the back of each piece. When the king was confronted with a question that called for divination, he first directed the question to, and beseeched the guidance of either Shang-ti (the Shang supreme deity) or his own royal ancestors. A diviner then applied a red-hot piece of tinder to one of the depressions. Within a few minutes, the heat caused the thin bone at the base of the depression to crack. The diviner then read these cracks to interpret the answer of the spirit, and thus determined what course of action the king should take.

Modern research shows that the pattern of cracks can be influenced by both the quantity of heat and the direction in which it is applied. If this is true, it is then conceivable that the diviners controlled many of the important affairs of the Shang state. However, records indicate that royal diviners were frequently executed (sometimes along with their families) for inaccuracy.

*All of the oracle bones on display at the National Palace Museum are on loan from the Academia Sinica.

Turtle Plastron

Following divination, the king's inquiry was written in ink on the front face of the bone. This was then carved into the bone, establishing what is now one of the most enduring records of the ancient past. The delicate cracks seen on this plastron are the result of additional incising used to clarify the original fire-induced cracks. The inquiry, concerning whether or not the king should dispatch a general on a military campaign, is written in two versions on the left and right hand sides of the plastron. The two versions of the question are posed in positive and negative (yes and no) forms, respectively.

Just as we read fate in the lines of a human palm, the Shang relied on the lines in the bones to make important decisions. In the end we do not know whether or not the king sent the general, but perhaps the fate of many men was determined by this small piece of shell.

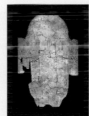 

Turtle plastron, Shang dynasty

Cattle scapula , Shang dynasty

Cattle Scapula

Due to the importance of divinatory ceremonies in the king's administration of the state, the bones used in these ceremonies were of exceptional value. This is evidenced by the fact that several small neighboring kingdoms are recorded to have offered turtles as tribute to the Shang. It is possible that the Shang court had a department exclusively responsible for storing and preparing divinatory shells and bones. This cattle scapula bears the records of a number of seperate spirit consultations, several of which include the name of the inscriber. By recording the inquiries of the ruler on the bones, these inscribers acted in a manner similar to the historians of later eras.

Painting and Calligraphy

The unique art of Chinese painting and calligraphy has, for centuries, relied on the use of a round-tipped brush as the fundamental means of applying ink. The experience and aesthetic sensation of using this brush in writing naturally influenced its use in painting. The National Palace Museum's collection of painting and calligraphy, which combines ten centuries of imperial acquisitions with the purchases and gifts of the past decades, numbers over ten thousand pieces. The collection contains works by virtually every famous painter and calligrapher in Chinese history, and is rightfully called a treasury of Chinese culture. Some of the most famous works in the collection include Wang Hsi-chih's *Clearing After Snowfall*, Yen Chen-ch'ing's *Draft Manuscript of a Memorial to My Nephew*, Fan K'uan's *Travelers Among Mountains and Streams*, and Kuo Hsi's *Early Spring*.

The Art of Brush and Ink

Chinese characters originally began as pictographic illustrations. Thus, their forms were determined not only by a practical need to record information, but also by aesthetic considerations. In other words, characters, as illustration, served as a vehicle for artistic expression— the products of which stand today as one of the hallmarks of East Asian art. From an artistic perspective, the unique combinations of structure, shape and line that define individual characters can be seen as formal prototypes. It is the many manipulations of these prototypes over the past several thousand years that defines the history of Chinese calligraphy and the scope of its aesthetic appeal.

The Museum's rich collection of calligraphy includes original masterpieces from the Chin and T'ang to Ming and Ch'ing dynasties. The majority of these works were originally part of the imperial palace collection that has been passed down over the centuries, and are thus well documented in textual records. The collection includes many works important to the history of Chinese calligraphy, which provide classical models for aesthetic appreciation and demonstrate the development of the art during each period of Chinese history.

Wei and Chin Dynasty Calligraphy

During the period known as the Six Dynasties, which essentially encompasses the third to sixth centuries A.D., the art of writing began to diversify into different calligraphic scripts. This diversification, driven by the master calligraphers of the age, would have a profound influence on the subsequent history of Chinese calligraphy. Around the third century A.D., the evolution of these various calligraphic scripts gradually came to a halt and were codified into what are known today as standard, running, and cursive scripts. During the fourth century Eastern Chin period, writing for everyday purposes, such as letters and essays, was predominantly done in the semi-cursive and cursive scripts. The noble class was particularly selective and fastidious in their appreciation of calligraphy and its styles; for them, it served an aesthetic as well as a functional purpose. The greatest master of the fourth century was the calligrapher Wang Hsi-chih. Born into a family of calligraphers, he became not only the most famous artist of his own day, but indeed the most influential calligrapher in all of Chinese history.

Chin dynasty Wang Hsi-chih

Clearing After Snowfall

Wang Hsi-chih (303-361) was a master calligrapher of unrivalled achievement and longstanding influence. The brushwork seen here possesses a soft, rounded resiliency and classical elegance, which reveals a sense of unaffected introspection. Titles of Wang Hsi-chih's works often include the character *tieh* (model), indicating that later calligraphers and collectors considered them worthy models for copying. Wang's reputation as the "Sage of Calligraphy" stems from his creation of the free, unrestrained quality that characterizes running script.

This work is a letter that Wang wrote to his friend Chang Hou, describing the clear sky after a snowfall. It expresses both Wang's longing for his distant friend and his wish for Chang's good fortune. Wang's calligraphy embodies the elegant and casual demeanor of a learned man. In writing a simple letter he does not adopt a deliberate artfulness, but rather, by means of mild and natural characters, reveals the daily workings of his emotions. Many connoisseurs believe that Chinese calligraphy can only achieve true aesthetic excellence when written in this sort of non-deliberate manner. *Clearing After Snowfall* was one of the most prized possessions of the Ch'ing imperial court, designated by the Ch'ien-lung emperor as one of the three heirlooms to be stored in the aptly named *Hall of the Three Rarities*.

Clearing After Snowfall, Wang Hsi-chih, Chin dynasty

羲之頓首 快雪時晴佳想

安善未果為結

力不次王

羲之頓首

山陰張侯

君倩

T'ang Calligraphy

The T'ang dynasty was a time of imperial strength and achievement in art and literature. It stands today as the golden age of Chinese calligraphy. Of the various well-established writing styles, standard script enjoyed the greatest popularity, and was practiced by one generation of calligraphers after another. The mid-T'ang is also famous for the powerful and liberated quality of its cursive script, which developed into a distinct style known as "wild cursive."

T'ang dynasty Huai Su

Autobiography

Huai Su (725-785) was a monk with a flamboyant personality who loved to drink wine, a proclivity that earned him the nickname "wild monk." When drunk, he was often inspired to write poems or compose essays. In *Autobiography*, he describes his experience of writing "wild cursive," and comments on the critiques of several of his contemporaries. Autobiography represents the free and open spirit of T'ang calligraphy, in contrast to the strict, rigorous training typically associated with this art form. Here, calligraphy takes on an improvisational nature, invoking the spirit of modern abstract art.

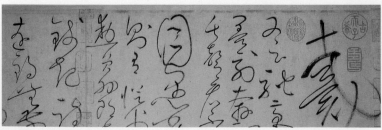

Autobiography (detail), Huai Su, T'ang dynasty

Yen Chen-ch'ing

Draft Manuscript of a Memorial to My Nephew

Yen Chen-ch'ing (709-785) is doubtless the most famous representative of the mid-T'ang school of calligraphy. Born to a prominent family, he endured over fifty years of the hardships and turmoil in government service, earning a lasting name as a forthright and honest official.

The *Draft Manuscript of a Memorial to My Nephew* is Yen's best surviving running script composition. Written in 758, the manuscript records Yen's sorrow upon learning of his nephew's untoward death in the recent, catastrophic An Lushan rebellion. Yen poured his heart's blood into the piece, spilling out his anguish and pain in tormented brushwork that lurches across the page.

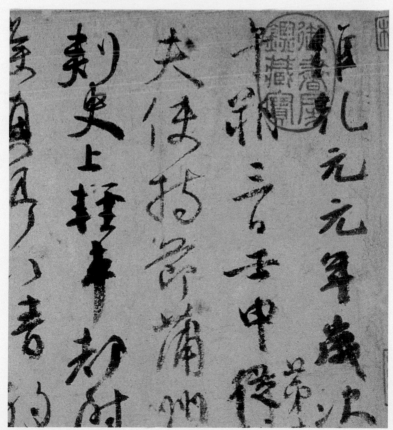

Draft Manuscript of a Memorial to My Nephew (detail),Yen Chen-ch'ing, T'ang dynasty

The Golden Age
of Sung Calligraphy

The Northern Sung (960-1127) was another highpoint in the history of Chinese calligraphy. During the Sung, the development of printing spurred the production and study of model calligraphy books, which remained the dominant force in calligraphic education through the seventeenth century. There is a famous phrase that reads, "Men of the Chin esteemed rhyme, men of the T'ang esteemed method, and men of the Sung esteemed intention." Essentially, one can interpret this as encapsulating the dominant aesthetic trend of each respective period. The Chin valued rhythm and rhyme, the T'ang pursued rules and standards, and the Sung honored personal expression. Therefore, each period inherited, but was not limited by, the achievements of the preceding age.

The Sung dynasty is most famous for its running script, which captured the individual expressionism of this "Age of Intent." Ts'ai Hsiang (1012-1067), Su Shih (1036-1101), Huang T'ing-chien (1045-1105), and Mi Fu (1051-1107) are remembered as the "Four Master Calligraphers of the Sung." They were officials, poets, and connoisseurs who, in pursuing their own individual modes of expression, together shaped the classic ideal of literati art. Ts'ai Hsiang wrote with regulated classicism, his strokes mild and amiable. Su Shih sought untrammeled freedom and spontaneity, claiming that his goal was to write with a spirit unburdened by technique. Huang T'ing-chien wrote with long, downward sweeping strokes, like a boatman pulling at oars with force and vigor. Mi Fu excelled at strong brushwork, his strokes like sweeping blades and taut bowstrings.

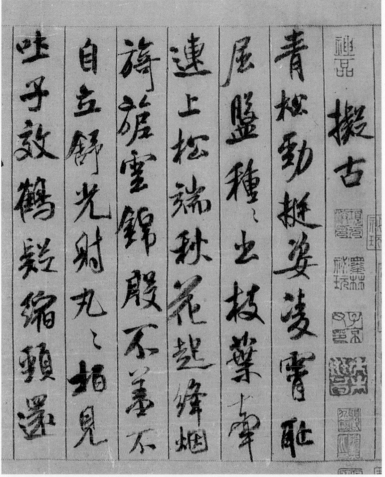

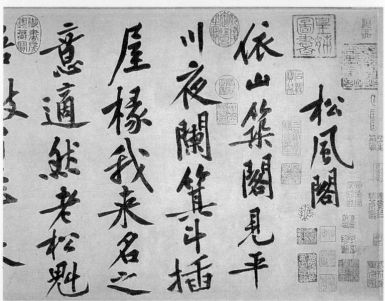

Above: On Szechwan Silk (detail), Mi Fu, Sung dynasty
Below: The Sung-feng ko Verse (detail), Huang T'ing-chien, Sung dynasty

水雲裏空庖煮寒菜

破竈燒濕葦那

知是寒食但見烏

The Cold Food Observance

Su Shih (1036-1101), also known as Su Tung-p'o, is a legendary, ageless figure in the history of Chinese literature, calligraphy, and painting. He valued personal, emotive expression and refused to succumb to the rules and standards of others. His taste in clothing and food left its mark on history, echoed today in such things as Tung-p'o Pork and the Tung-p'o Shawl.

In *The Cold Food Observance*, Su describes his thoughts while exiled on the frontier of civilized China, his brush imbued with sonorous emotion. Su's ink flows with abandon, at times smooth and strong, at others raw and lurching, as he fashions characters that grow and shirk and lines that thicken and thin in a melody of slow acceleration and sudden conclusion. The piece is thus a classic example of the "lyrical" quality that characterizes and denotes Su's masterpieces.

The scroll was originally part of the Ch'ing imperial collection, yet after the sack of the Peking Summer Palace by French and British forces in 1860, it fell into private hands. During the Tung-chih reign (1862-74), it entered the collection of a Kwangtung man named Feng, where it narrowly avoided destruction in a fire that left some traces along its lower edge. Later, the scroll was taken to Japan, where it weathered both earthquakes and bombing during the Second World War. After the war, a Taipei collector obtained the scroll, and only in recent years has the masterpiece found its way back into the collection of the Palace Museum. The scroll is famed as one of Su's greatest works, and its return to the Museum is certainly an auspicious omen and cause for celebration.

The Cold Food Observance (detail), Su Shih, Sung dynasty

The Antiquarian Style
of the Yüan

The Sung-era "calligraphy of intention" grew excessive and moribund during the later half of the dynasty. In the Yüan dynasty (1279-1368), Chinese calligraphy underwent another transformation as calligraphers turned back to the "ancient methods" of the Chin and T'ang eras. The most famous calligrapher of the age was Chao Meng-fu. A skilled poet, essayist, and painter, Chao possessed a lovely, elegant calligraphic style that exerted a profound influence on later generations, particularly those of the late Yüan and early Ming.

Yüan dynasty Chang Yü
Seven Character Regulated Verse

Chang Yü (1277-1348), a native of Ch'ien-tang in Chekiang, was a famous Taoist priest of the Mao-shan sect who created refined and elegant paintings and calligraphy. At the age of sixty, he abandoned the Taoist order for a return to his Confucian roots. He spent the remainder of his life wandering in the Chekiang and Kiangsu region, collaborating with local artists and scholars. With extensive literary training and calligraphic skill, Chang was well known in the Taoist, Buddhist, and literati circles of the Yüan dynasty. At one point, he studied calligraphy under the master Chao Meng-fu. Chang Yü's calligraphic style was generally clear, relaxed, and lively, yet portions of this piece are written in a more precise and mannerly fashion. This combination of different writing styles in a single work demonstrates his mastery of the calligraphic craft.

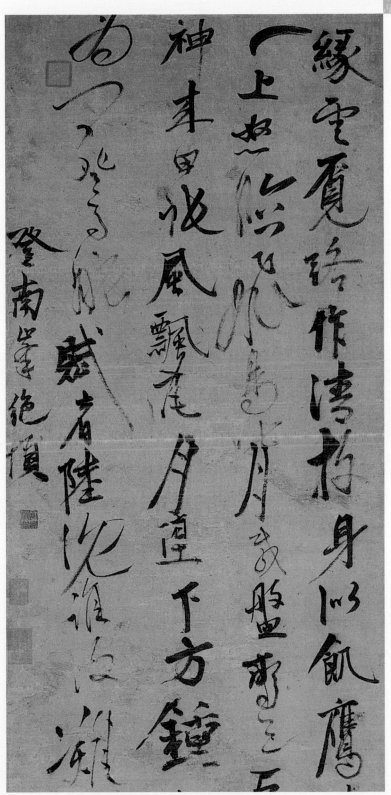

Seven Character Regulated Verse (detail), Chang Yü, Yüan dynasty

Chao Meng-fu

Former and Latter Odes on the Red Cliff

The antiquarian approach to calligraphy during the Yüan dynasty saw the ascendancy of the elegant and upright styles of the Chin and T'ang dynasties. Chao Meng-fu (1254-1322), one of the most famous men of the age, was regarded by many as the greatest calligrapher since Yen Chen-ch'ing. A descendent of the Sung royal family, Chao was a master wordsmith who was summoned to the court of the first Yüan emperor Khubilai Khan. There he served in important official posts, rising to the prestigious rank of Hanlin Academician.

Chao Meng-fu's calligraphy combines the various achievements of his predecessors. By straddling the boundary between standard and running scripts, his writing, at once proper and luxurious, reaches for the classic brushwork of Wang Hsi-chih. Limited by the strictures of official life, Chao found release in artistic expressions of his longing for retirement to an idyllic lifestyle in the countryside. This longing fits perfectly with the eremitic theme of Su Tung-p'o's *Odes to the Red Cliff*, which Chao copies with flying, moist strokes that sweep in natural euphoria across the page. In his brushwork, one finds a lasting adoration for Su's insights into the meaning of life.

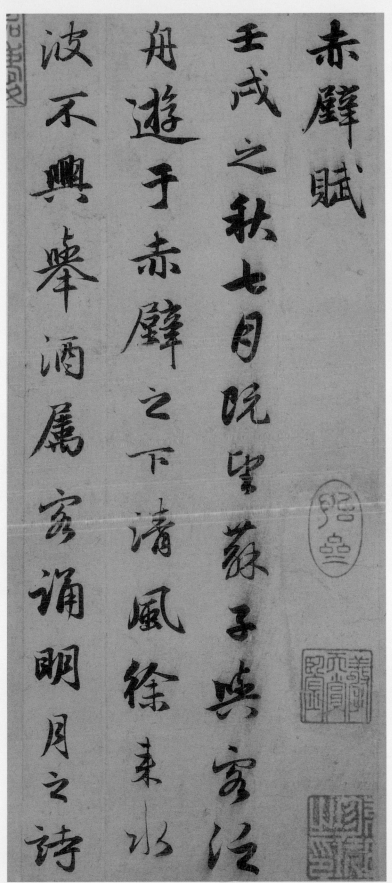

赤壁賦

壬戌之秋七月既望蘇子與客泛
舟遊于赤壁之下清風徐來水
波不興舉酒屬客誦明月之詩

Former and Latter Odes on the Red Cliff (detail), Chao Meng-fu, Yüan dynasty

Ming and Ch'ing Stele and Copybook Calligraphy

During the middle years of the Ming dynasty, a group of famous artists, including such luminaries as Shen Chou, Chu Yün-ming, Wen Chengming and T'ang Yin, transformed their home city of Soochow, located in the Chiang-nan region of the lower Yangtze, into the most thriving cultural center of sixteenth century China. In the waning years of the Ming dynasty, a new figure named Tung Ch'i-ch'ang entered onto the Chiang-nan scene. A masterful connoisseur, copyist, and innovator, Tung exerted a powerful influence on the aesthetic theory and calligraphic style of the late Ming and early Ch'ing dynasties.

The seventeenth century saw the emergence of two competing approaches to calligraphy. On one side were those who emphasized the styles found on ancient steles, which were disseminated through rubbings. On the other side were those who took their models from the copybook (t'ieh) tradition. Since the Ch'ing imperial court largely followed the lead of Tung Ch'i-ch'ang (1555-1636) in promoting the copybook tradition, the Museum's collection of later calligraphy is dominated by artists of this latter faction. In the mid-Ch'ing, the study of ancient bronze inscriptions, steles, and seals began to have a strong influence on calligraphic practice. A new aesthetic preference for primitive, antiquarian script replaced the earlier Ming dynasty style, which prized delicacy and elegance.

The Pai-yü shan Poem (detail), Tung Ch'i-ch'ang, Ming dynasty

感遇賦　　　張九齡

開元二十四年夏盛暑勅賜

齡與馬立陸田耆時而用

江湖之六方安知順景而

Chu Yün-ming

Seven Character Regulated Verse

Chu Yün-ming (1460-1562), a native of Soochow, was born with an extra finger, a deformity for which he gave himself the nickname "Branched Finger." A highly accomplished scholar, skilled in all four traditional calligraphic scripts, Chu Yün-ming was said to have "...left nothing unlearned and nothing unachieved." The "wild calligraphy" of his later years is famed for its endless variation and hailed as the finest of the Ming dynasty. Chu Yün-ming's unique cursive is characterized by its unusual combination of several different styles within the same work. The present scroll demonstrates this mastery of variation. Chu's brush sprints across the page, forging characters that invade the domain of their neighbors and lines that tumble in on each other in a cacophony of dense breathlessness. Yet at the same time, the brush strokes break free in sweeping waves to the left and right. Some lines number only two or three characters, some break off abruptly, and some bind together in a great meddle, creating a powerful contrast that casts off all bounds of restraint and soars free.

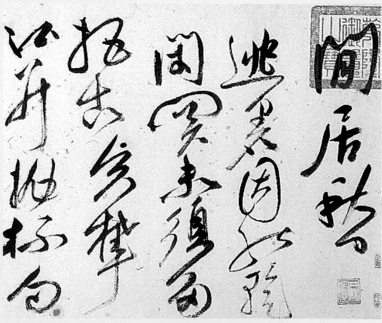

Seven Character Regulated Verse (detail), Chu Yün-ming, Ming dynasty

Running Standard Script

Liu Yung (1719-1804) was a successful candidate in the palace examinations who became a high ranking official under the emperor Ch'ien-lung. He was highly skilled in calligraphy, and was well known for his administrative and literary accomplishments. During the formative years of his calligraphy education, he followed the styles of the Yüan and Ming dynasty calligraphy masters Tung Ch'i-ch'ang and Chao Meng-fu, which were in fashion at the time. In his later years, Liu Yung focused his attention on masters of the Chin, T'ang, and Sung dynasties. He was particularly captivated by the writing styles of Yen Chen-ch'ing and Su Shih, and incorporated much of their tech-nique into his own mature style. This piece, written in a bold and stately manner, meets the standards of the ancient masters, and is a fine example of Liu Yung's distinctive style.

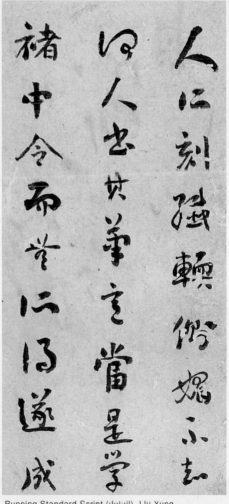

Running Standard Script (detail), Liu Yung, Ch'ing dynasty

T'ang Painting

The subject matter of T'ang painting centered on human life, often describing legends or historical events. As seen in the work A Palace Concert, Tang artists also depicted the lifestyles and social interactions of women—specifically those of the imperial court.

T'ang China was a multicultural melting pot. Painting styles of the time reflect this diversity, and emphasize grand and dignified themes. For example, T'ang landscape painters generally worked in what are known as the "blue-and-green" and "gold-and-green" landscape styles. Both terms derive from the use of bright, vibrant color to create an aura of grandeur and dignity.

A Palace Concert

In this scene, female court musicians gather around a square table after a banquet. Some pluck the *pipa*, while others play the *cheng* (a type of string instrument) and the wooden flute; a few listen intently and keep the beat with pieces of wood. The atmosphere exudes a sense of concentration and harmony, as a cooperative group effort was necessary in order to play well and win the emperor's approval.

The detail of the painting is astounding. In the left corner the artist has placed a young servant girl who is waiting upon the ladies, while underneath the table sits a small dog, enjoying the view. The meticulous detail presented in this and other depictions of court life is an important source of information for modern historians. Paintings like this inform us of such things as the hairstyles and clothing fashions of the time.

The materials used to color the painting, as well as the plump forms of the court women, indicate that this particular work was created in the late T'ang.

A Palace Concert (detail), T'ang dynasty

Five Dynasties Painting

The Five Dynasties period (907-960) was a turning point in the history of Chinese painting. In both Szechwan and the Chiang-nan region of the lower Yangtze, local talent, combined with imperial patronage, brought new vitality to the arts. The period saw developments in the landscape, bird-and-flower, figure, religious, and other genres of Chinese painting. At the court of the Southern T'ang (937-975), the establishment of an official painting academy signaled a new imperial involvement in the arts that would play a critical role in the painting of the subsequent Sung dynasty. The Five Dynasties not only inherited the traditions of the T'ang, but also laid the foundation for the stellar achievements of the Sung.

Five Dynasties

Herd of Deer in a Maple Grove

This is one of the most unique surviving paintings of the Five Dynasties period. With its amalgamation of various painting methods and stark contrasts in style, the work presents a striking image. The deer have visible shadows and bodies that possess a great sense of volume. The appearance of physical solidity was obtained by using light, nearly transparent ink to outline the form, followed by darker ink to fill in the body. As a result, the deer lack distinct outlines, giving them a rounded, three-dimensional quality.

A maple forest, painted in the mixed colors of early autumn, acts as a decorative backdrop for the deer. The intersection of lines and colors gives the scene an indistinct luminance, while the white outlining of the green leaves imbues the forest with a rich and fertile vibrancy.

Herd of Deer in a Maple Grove, Five Dynasties

Chü Jan

Layered Peaks and Dense Forests

Chü Jan was a great landscape painter born in Chung-ling, Kiangsi, in the tenth century. Early in life, he lived as a monk at the K'ai-yüan Temple, yet eventually departed to become the apprentice of the master landscape painter Tung Yüan (ca. early tenth century). Building upon the hemp-fiber texture strokes (a technique of representing irregular surfaces) of his master, Chü developed his own distinctive style of layered-peak landscapes.

Chü Jan painted chunks of stone stacked atop one another to represent mountain peaks. These chunks of stone came to be known as "alum heads," or *fan-t'ou* in Chinese. Atop the alum heads, Chü added dense drops of black ink to represent small trees and grass. This technique, combined with the hemp-fiber texture strokes, brilliantly captured the essence and grandeur of China's mountain and forest landscapes. In gazing upon this work, one can almost feel the vitality of nature emanating from the scene.

Chü's style was to have a major impact on future generations of Chinese painters, most notably the so-called "Four Masters of the Yüan dynasty."

Sung Dynasty Painting

The art of Chinese painting reached its zenith during the Sung Dynasty. This was true of naturalistic bird-and-flower painting, genre scenes of playing children and peddlers, and, most importantly, monumental "mind landscapes" of mountains, forests, and streams.

The Sung Painting Academy was a crucial force in the advancement of painting, particularly during the early twelfth century reign of the emperor Hui-tsung. A talented painter in his own right, Hui-tsung reorganized the Academy and recruited painters from across China through an examination system similar to that used to select government officials. He divided the studying of painting into six genres: Buddhism, portraiture, landscape, birds and beasts, flowers and bamboo, and architecture. He also elevated the social status of Academy painters by bestowing them with generous support and honors.

Northern Sung dynasty Fan K'uan

Travelers Among Mountain and Streams

This work, in which the artist uses strong brushstrokes to depict the majestic mountain ranges of northern China, is perhaps the finest extant masterpiece of early Northern Sung landscape painting.

While the lower third of the painting is occupied by a scene of travelers moving along a narrow trail, the primary focus of the work lies instead on the towering mountain peak that dominates the remaining two-thirds of the painting. To enhance the awe-inspiring grandeur of the mountain, Fan K'uan (fl. 990-1030) painted the party of travelers, secluded dwellings, forest, and other details in a minute scale that juxtaposes the peak and elevates it into the heavens. Between the crevices of the cliff flows a waterfall, its mist enshrouding the foot of mountain, concealing its foundation and accentuating its breathtaking majesty.

The cliffs that dominate the work are clearly outlined and filled in with so-called "rain drop" texture stokes, which communicate a sense of stony solidity. By maintaining a consistently exaggerated contrast of large and small, high and low elements, Fan keeps the viewer's attention focused on the immense and eternal nature of the mountain.

Travelers Among Mountain and Streams, Fan K'uan, Northern Sung dynasty

樹綠藂藂溪
閒凍樓閣仙
居家上層不
藉物栖閒絃
微妻山早見
氣如茶
己卯春月
尚題

Northern Sung dynasty Kuo Hsi

Early Spring

Kuo Hsi (ca.1020-1100) was the most important landscape painter of the mid to late Northern Sung dynasty. His defining masterpiece, Early Spring, is one of the earliest examples of a signed work bearing the author's name, a title, and the date of completion.

To recreate the atmosphere of early spring, Kuo Hsi carefully observed the seasonal changes of the natural environment. In this scene, the ice on the ground has begun to melt, the trees are sprouting, and a dewy freshness resonates in the morning air. Using layer upon layer of watery ink, Kuo Hsi constructed billowing rock formations which were extensively copied by later painters and eventually came to be known as "cloud head" texture stokes. The dominant central peak lies on the painting's vertical axis, with smaller hills and clouds interspersed below and to the sides, giving the image a sense of movement and vitality.

The trees in Early Spring are skillfully described with varying brushstrokes and shades of ink, in a manner that contrasts sharply with the simpler, more formulaic methods of later painters.

The artist's inscription lies on the left side of the scroll. It reads, "Early Spring, painted in the Jen Tzu year (A.D. 1072) by Kuo Hsi." In the upper right corner is a poem about the dawning of spring, composed by the Ch'ing emperor Ch'ien-lung in tribute to Kuo Hsi's masterpiece. Early Spring and Travelers Among Mountains and Streams, are together considered the twin pillars of Northern Sung landscape painting.

Left: Early Spring, Kuo Hsi, Northern Sung dynasty
Above: Emperor Ch'ien-lung's inscription on Kuo Hsi's Early Spring

Wen T'ung

Ink Bamboo

Wen T'ung (1018-1079) was a scholar known for both his literary talents and artistic genius. His elegant and masculine brushwork found its highest expression in the depiction of bamboo.

Bamboo, with its hollow and segmented structure, is traditionally associated in China with the humble and honest scholar-gentleman. In Chinese, the word for hollow is also used to communicate humility, while the word *chieh* (bamboo segment) also means propriety and good conduct. Therefore, Wen T'ung's decision to depict bamboo is highly symbolic, particularly given the fact that he painted it at the height of his official career. The body and stem of the bamboo are drawn with thick, heavy brushstrokes, in contrast with the light shade of ink used for the leaves. This lively painting style had an immense impact on Chinese art, marking the beginning of the division between professional and scholarly painting. The style developed by scholar-amateurs, who painted as a mode of intellectual expres-sion, became increas-ingly independent of the traditional painting styles practiced by professionals, who sought contracts and commissions.

Ink Bamboo, Wen T'ung, Sung dynasty

Sung dynasty Liang K'ai

Splashed Ink Immortal

The early thirteenth century artist Liang K'ai, also known as "Crazy Liang," served as a painter-in-attendance in the Southern Sung court of Emperor Ning-tsung, where he specialized in landscape, Buddhist subjects, and images of ghosts and spirits.

The drunken figure in this painting appears to be bathed in ink. Although his head and features are thinly outlined, his body is splashed out across the page in great swathes of wet ink that express the misty and ephemeral quality of a drunken immortal, hobbling through the ether. The figure's squinting eyes, flowing beard, broad nose, and pursed lips communicate a sense of inebriated ease and contentment. This is not a common drunk from the streets, but rather an otherworldly incarnation, wandering on the bounds of physical reality.

In Sung painting, artists strove to capture the "likeness" of their subject matter. Yet with the growing influence of Ch'an Buddhist philosophy in the thirteenth century, painters gradually gave up the effort to observe and thereby capture reality, turning instead to an introspective approach driven purely by instinct, intellect, and intuition. The present work is an excellent example of this new trend.

Splashed Ink Immortal, Liang K'ai, Sung dynasty

73

Ma Yüan

On a Mountain Path in Spring

Ma Yüan (fl. ca. 1190-1224), a member of the famous Ma family of painters, served as a painter-in-attendance in the Painting Academy under two Southern Sung emperors, Kuang-tsung and Ning-tsung (1190-1224). For the subject matter of his scenic paintings, Ma often chose the Southern Sung capital, Lin-an, located on the site of present day Hangchow. He was known for a unique style of asymmetrical composition which located the focus of the scene in a single corner of the painting, while leaving the remainder of the composition largely empty. The style earned him the epithet "One Corner Ma."

Sung paintings often give viewers the impression that they are looking upon the visual depiction of a poem. This lyrical quality is readily apparent in the present image of a springtime landscape in southern China. The cool breeze and clear skies ease the heart of a scholar traveling along a mountain path. Accompanied by a servant boy bearing his zither, the man pauses to admire the freshness and vitality of his surroundings. A willow tree, its draping branches green with budding leaves, invites a pair of happily chirping orioles. The mood of the scene is aptly reflected in the verse inscribed by Emperor Ning-tsung in the upper left-hand corner of the work.

It is said that the Sung emperors often tested Academy painters by presenting them with a poetic phrase, which they were asked to depict visually. At other times, poems were added after the painting's completion. In either case, the poem and painting complement and mutually enhance one another. The present work is an excellent case in point.

Ma Yüan's simple and refreshing style had a profound effect on his successors. With limited strokes, his work succeeds at creating a poetic space that animates our emotions.

On a Mountain Path in Spring (detail), Ma Yüan, Sung dynasty

Yüan Dynasty Painting

Painting took on a more somber tone during the Yüan dynasty, as the Mongol conquerors of China oppressed and persecuted the scholarly elite of the fallen Sung dynasty. Since explicit writing was forbidden, many scholars withdrew into hermitage and used painting as their only method of expression.

The most influential artist of the Yüan was the scholar, painter, and calligrapher Chao Meng-fu (1254-1322). Chao worked in a "scholarly" style that was adopted and practiced by most later Yüan artists, including the Four Great Masters: Huang Kung-wang, Wu Chen, Ni Tsan, and Wang Meng. Chao's style and approach to painting continued to exert a powerful influence in the Ming and Ch'ing dynasties.

Autumn Colors on the Ch'üeh and Hua Mountains (detail), Chao Meng-fu, Yüan dynasty

Yüan dynasty Wu Chen

Fishermen

Wu Chen (1280-1354) lived a life of poverty and destitution, eking out a living as an occasional fortuneteller. Like many other educated scholars forced to endure the oppression of Mongol overlords, Wu eventually withdrew to the countryside for anonymity and safety.

Wu Chen's landscape painting reflects his honest, simple, and sincere nature. In this painting, he uses thick, dark ink to describe the stones at the river's edge. A winding path passes a pavilion, overlooked by a pair of towering, windswept trees, and wanders down to the water. A river extends off toward the horizon, its banks cloaked with dense reeds, the rippling of its distant waters sparkling in the sunlight. Across the undulating waters comes a small covered boat with a young servant boy at its helm. The boy's master sits in the bow of the boat, his arms wrapped around his knees and his gaze fixed on the distant shore. On the far bank, mountains rise up high into the sky, their summits cloaked in a dense mist that obscures the buildings nestled in the hills. This quiet and secluded world represents a refuge for the downtrodden and unwanted scholar.

Fishermen, Wu Chen, Yüan dynasty

Yüan dynasty Ni Tsan

The Jung-hsi Studio

Ni Tsan (1301-1374) was born into a wealthy family in the prosperous, fertile eastern region of Kiangsu. Of the four Great Masters of the Yüan, Ni's painting style is particularly neat and unadorned. He regarded himself a lofty scholar, removed from the travails of common men. Famous for his irrational fear of uncleanness, Ni expressed his phobias with the brush, sketching out clean and unsoiled worlds with only a minimal repertoire of sharp, dry brushstrokes. Unlike the painting of earlier dynasties, Yüan landscape no longer strove for realism, but rather served as an outlet for the scholar to express his intellect and emotions.

The present work was a gift from Ni to his friend, the doctor Jen-chung. The title, Jung-hsi Studio, is taken from the name of Jen-chung's residence. Of course, Ni's representation of the studio is largely symbolic, for the only building in the painting is a simple pavilion. Yüan literati artists frequently used painting as a vehicle for sharing their emotions with friends and providing, through landscape, a meditative sanctuary from the concerns of daily life.

The Jung-hsi Studio, Ni Tsan, Yüan dynasty

Southern Branches in the Early Spring

Wang Mien (1287-1359), though born into a rural family of farmers, studied intensely to prepare for the civil service examination that would allow him to pursue a career as a scholar-official. Despite his efforts, he failed to pass the exam, and instead lived much of his life in anonymity.

Selling his paintings to make a living, he eventually became famous for his pictures of plum trees.

The single plum branch in this painting is aged, but still full of vitality. It curves and bends, with smaller stems shooting for the sky and an abundance of plum blossoms, outlined in thin lines of ink, bursting forth in a flourishing array.

Wang inscribed the work with a poem that describes the plum tree's proud, solitary strength, and by implication, the austerity and unbroken will of scholars like himself. This work, completed in 1352, is an excellent example of the painting style that Wang cultivated in his later years.

Southern Branches in the Early Spring,
Wang Mien, Yüan dynasty

Ming Dynasty Painting

The Ming dynasty marked a return to native Han rule, a point which the Ming government sought to emphasize by reviving the artistic traditions of the Han, T'ang, and Sung dynasties. The court painters of the early Ming deliberately renounced the influences of the Yüan literati, and turned instead to painters of the Southern Sung, such as Ma Yüan and Hsia Kuei, for inspiration.

During the middle years of the Ming dynasty, a new movement, which eventually became known as the Che school, began to emerge in the coastal regions of Chekiang and Fukien. The Che painters continued to pursue the naturalistic approach of the Sung, but in a more expansive and unrestrained manner. At the same time, another group of painters centered in Kiangsu began to coalesce into the so-called Wu school. Taking their lead from the Great Masters of the Yüan, the Wu painters emphasized classical tradition and the expression of lofty literati ideals.

The late Ming was a time of great transformation in Chinese society. Conservative, orthodox elements promoted the antiquarian resurrection of earlier painting styles, while other, more individualistic painters like Hsü Wei (1521-1593) boldly experimented with the expressive dimensions of ink. In the midst of this tumult, the great artist and connoisseur Tung Ch'i-ch'ang established a redefined set of aesthetic criteria for the judgment of Chinese art.

Left: Egrets and Hibiscus in Autumn, Lü-chi (1477-?), Ming dynasty
Right: Pomegranate, Hsü Wei, Ming dynasty

T'ang Yin

Sound of the Pines
Along a Mountain Path

T'ang Yin (1470-1523), a member of the Wu school, was a gifted and intelligent man of dashing manner and refined bearing. He served as an official under the Hung-chih emperor, but lost his position after being implicated in a civil service examination cheating scheme. The scandal led T'ang Yin to abandon political life and take up the art of painting as a full-time endeavor under the tutelage of Chou Ch'en.

T'ang Yin is quite possibly the best known of all Ming painters. Colorful stories of his dashing (some would say reckless) behavior are a long-standing part of Chinese popular tradition. Though the veracity of many of these tales is open to doubt, they nevertheless give us a general sense of the free-spirited character of this unique artist.

T'ang Yin completed this monumental work at the age of forty-seven. The distant mountains are painted in a light ink wash, giving the scene a sense of peace and tranquility. In the foreground, a scholar, trailed by a young servant bearing a zither, meanders along a path, lost in the sounds of a gurgling spring and the wind in the pines. In its exquisite blending of technical skill and introspective lyricism, the work serves as an excellent example of Ming dynasty literati painting.

Sound of the Pines Along a Mountain Path, T'ang Yin, Ming dynasty

女几山前野路横松聲偏合泉聲

靜裏閒傾耳便覺冲然道氣生

孝父母大人先生 治下唐寅畫呈

Wen Cheng-ming

Winter Spring by the Ancient Tree

Wen Cheng-ming (1470-1559), born in Ch'ang-chou, Kiangsu, lived to the venerable age of ninety. In his twenties, he sought out the master Shen Chou to learn the art of painting. As a member of the Wu school, Shen taught him that the aim of painting was not to make the most accurate copy of a worldly object, but rather to express one's scholarly sensibilities and moral cultivation. The paintings of both Shen and Wen revolve around literati themes—attending elegant gatherings, composing poetry in a haze of inebriation, sipping tea on the banks of a stream, and the arrival and departure of old friends—which are frequently emphasized through the addition of a poem.

Within the narrow vertical space of this painting, an ancient cedar and old pine intertwine, backed by a stony cliff. A spring high up in the rocks sends a lively stream of water cascading down into the scene below.

Winter Spring by the Ancient Tree,
Wen Cheng-ming, Ming dynasty

Ch'ing Dynasty Painting

In the early Ch'ing dynasty, court painting continued in the tradition laid down by Tung Ch'i-ch'ang. The most representative artists in this category are the "Four Wangs"—Wang Shih-min, Wang Chien, Wang Hui, and Wang Yuan-ch'i—who together with Yun Shou-p'ing and Wu Li are collectively known as the "Six Masters of the Early Ch'ing."

Painters working outside of the court came largely from the ranks of dispossessed Ming loyalists, many of whom had lost family and property in the course of the Manchu invasion. Because many of these men sought solace in the monastery, it is unsurprising that one of the most famous groups of early Ch'ing artists was known as the "Four Monks": Pa Ta Shan Jen, Shih T'ao, Shih Hsi, and Chien Chiang. Another group, led by Kung Hsien, was known as the "Eight Masters of Chin ling." Similarly choosing to withdraw themselves from society, these artists retired to the countryside in the classic fashion of disaffected literati, communicating with one another through gifts of painting and poetry.

In addition to perpetuating earlier traditions, the Ch'ing Painting Academy was also heavily influenced by the European painting styles of the Jesuit artists working within the imperial court.

Ch'ing dynasty Shih T'ao

Landscape

Due to family misfortune, Shih T'ao (1642-ca.1707) was forced to join a monastery at a very young age. "Shih T'ao" is in fact his Buddhist name. He spent his life traveling through China, painting along the way to keep himself amused.

Literati painting in the Ming dynasty, burdened by the weight of tradition and school affiliation, left little room for independent self-expression. This changed with the Four Monks, who, in enduring the hardships of a tumultuous age, shirked the standards of the past and developed their own distinctive styles. Though grouped together, each of the Four Monks pursued their own unique paths. Shih T'ao himself worked in a particularly free and unconventional manner, developing an individual style that remains instantly recognizable to this day.

An exceptional landscape painter, he also excelled at depicting the four plants that most symbolize the Chinese scholar: plum, orchid, bamboo, and chrysanthemum. Shih T'ao experimented with a variety of techniques; from thin, carefully articulated linework to bold splashes of heavy black ink and even applications of bright color. He frequently added his own or earlier poems to his paintings, which represent some of the most successful fusions of the three arts of poetry, calligraphy, and painting.

Landscape, Shih T'ao, Ch'ing dynasty

Yün Shou-p'ing

Peonies

A learned man of high integrity, Yün Shou-ping (1633-1690) was not only a skilled poet and essayist, but also famed as the finest flower painter of the early Ch'ing. He credited his focus on flowers to his friendship with Wang Hui. The story goes that Yün, after seeing Wang's brilliant landscape paintings, remarked that he could never paint landscape so well, and so turned to genre of flower painting.

The purple, red, and white peonies in this painting, painted in a "boneless" manner without outlines, are portrayed in both frontal and profile views. Yün uses shaded color to create the impression of layered petals, and delicate brushstrokes to draw the stems. Awash in flamboyant hues, the composition still succeeds in communicating a sense of elegance and dignity

Peonies, Yün Shou-p'ing, Ch'ing dynasty

Ch'ing dynasty Wang Yüan-ch'i
Poetry in Painting

The grandson of Wang Shih-ming, Wang Yüan-ch'i (1642-1715) was involved in authenticating the court's collection of painting and calligraphy. The youngest member of the Four Wangs, Wang Yüan-chi was also the most innovative and successful at breaking free from the Academy tradition.

Wang Yüan-ch'i's landscape takes inspiration from Yüan styles, as demonstrated here in his delicate brushwork, choice of color, and layered ink. The present painting is one of his finest surviving works.

Poetry in Painting, Wang Yüan-ch'i, Ch'ing dynasty

Ch'ing dynasty Lang Shih-ning (Giuseppe Castiglione)
A Hundred Fine Horses

Giuseppe Castiglione (1688-1766), an Italian Jesuit from Milan, arrived in China at the age of twenty-seven. He initially lived in Macau, where he learned to speak Chinese and familiarized himself with local customs, and then took up a post as a painter at the Ch'ing court, serving sequentially under the emperors Kang-hsi, Yung-cheng, and Ch'ien-lung. He eventually became known for his masterful treatment of human, flower, and animal subjects.

At the onset of his court career, Castiglione painted mainly in the Western tradition. However, through years of hard work, he mastered traditional Chinese painting methods and ultimately combined the two to create a fresh and innovative style.

The subjects of the present work, a hundred fine horses at pasture on the steppe, are shown in wide variety of postures. Every element in the painting is depicted with intense realism. Colors are bright, and the overall composition is highly complex. Completed in 1728, the painting is a classic example of Castiglione's early style.

A Hundred Fine Horses (detail), Lang Shih-ning (Giuseppe Castiglione), Ch'ing dynasty

Court painters

A City of Cathay

The earliest known version of this painting, a scene of busy urban life during the Tomb Sweeping festival, was painted during the Sung dynasty by the artist Chang Tse-tuan. In it, Chang captured the everyday life and customs of the Northern Sung capital at present-day Kaifeng. The work was a tour de force of high realism, and inspired many later copies. The most famous of these reproductions is the Ch'ing court copy seen here.

This collaborative work, produced by a group of five court painters, was completed in 1736. The copy combines the styles and features of previous versions with the unique customs and popular entertainments of the Ming and Ch'ing dynasties. These activities include such things as a theatrical performance, acrobatics, and a martial arts competition, the lively quality of which communicate the festive air of the scene.

Although this painting has lost much of the archaic tone of the Sung dynasty version, it is a valuable source of information on late Ming and early Ch'ing life and customs. The work also reflects the influence of Western techniques, which were popular in court painting at the time. The buildings and streets, for example, are rendered in single-point perspective, and one even can even discern European influence in some of the architectural details. The brilliant color and myriad array of exquisitely detailed figures and structures marks this work as one of the finest masterpieces of the Ch'ing court.

A City of Cathay (detail), Court painters, Ch'ing dynasty

Ceramics

Through experimentation, the people of ancient times gradually began to understand the properties of clay and develop techniques to mold and utilize it. After discovering that fired clay becomes a hard, durable material, they began using it to craft containers for holding and heating liquids. The production of pottery marks the beginnings of human civilization.

Porcelain is made by applying glaze to pure white kaolin clay, which is then fired at a high temperature. The result is a thin and hard jade-like substance, which resonates with a clear and crisp ring when tapped. Porcelain techniques developed gradually and attained maturity around the Sung dynasty, an era famous for the simple elegance of its white and celadon ceramics. Ceramic artistry attained its highest degree of technical perfection during the Ming and Ch'ing dynasties, when the wares of the official kilns at Ching-te-chen were exported to markets around the world. The admiration Europeans had for Chinese porcelain was so great that they applied the popular term for these wares—"China"—to their country of origin.

Painted earthenware jar

The Neolithic inhabitants of ancient China developed sophisticated methods for the firing and molding of clay. Early painted and burnished black earthenware represents the first peak in the history of Chinese ceramic art. The earthenware of the so-called "painted pottery cultures" of ancient Honan and Shansi is brick red in color, with a finely grained texture, lightly burnished surface, and painted designs in black, red, maroon, brown, and white. This style of pottery eventually spread to the regions of southern and eastern China, reaching even as far as Taiwan. This earthenware jar, dating to approximately 2000 B.C., features broad shoulders, a large torso, and a pair of handles placed roughly halfway up the body. Its full and sturdy form is enhanced by its simple design and the harmonious color of the spiraled geometric shapes that decorate its surface.

Green glazed ceramic model of a pavilion

During the Han dynasty, miniature clay figurines and models, replicating aspects of everyday life, were frequently buried with the dead to accompany them in the afterlife. The range of these figurines is immense, featuring everthing from servants to carriages and bands of musicians. Pottery burial objects also included symbols of wealth, such as livestock and miniature grain silos. Han tombs have also yielded models of many different types of buildings, which offer valuable information on the construction technology and architectural styles of the period. This green glazed tower is minutely detailed, with exquisite depictions of the windows, floors, balconies, and roof. The complexity of the building suggests that it was modeled after a structure owned by a member of the upper class.

Right: Green glazed ceramic model of a pavilion, Han dynasty
Left: Painted pottery vessel, Neolithic period

Celadon pi-hsieh screen holder

Images of mythical winged lions in Chinese art are derived from Assyrian and Persian influences that entered China around the beginning of the first millenium A.D. The Chinese named these animals *t'ien-lu* (bearers of bounty from heaven) or *pi-hsieh* (dispellers of evil) and regarded them as variants of traditional Chinese dragons and *ch'i-lin* (a unicorn-like creature of Chinese mythology). The top of this hollow piece bears a round hole, indicating that it may have once been used as the foot of a standing screen. Another interpretation is that it held water for dripping on an inkstone. The entire piece is covered with a thin and glossy layer of pale green glaze.

Celadon pi-hsieh screen holder, Western Chin dynasty

Tri-color glazed image of Virūdhaka

Tri-color glaze is one of the most distinctive characteristics of T'ang dynasty ceramics. To create a "tri-color" piece, T'ang potters first sculpted an earthenware body, over which they applied a layer of white slip (clay mixed with water). The piece was then decorated with three (or more) types of glaze, which were colored with such elements as copper, iron, manganese, and cobalt. To complete the process, the piece was then fired at a relatively low temperature of around eight hundred degrees celsius. During the T'ang, tri-color glaze was primarily used to decorate the many human and animal figurines, models of buildings, and replicas of everyday possessions, that were buried with the dead. By replicating the world of the living, these diverse items offer insight in the daily life of the T'ang dynasty, and serve as a virtual "encyclopedia" of the customs, clothing fashions, and artistic styles of the period. This enormous tri-color Virūdhaka once served as a tomb guardian used to ward off evil. The influence of Tang dynasty tri-colored pottery on later ceramic styles was immense. Foreign glazes, such as Persian tri-color, Islamic tri-color, and Thai tri-color, as well as the tri-color glazes of later Chinese dynasties, were all influenced by this T'ang dynasty style.

Tri-color glazed image of Virūdhaka, T'ang dynasty

Sung Dynasty Ceramics

The Sung imperial court valued elegant, refined art, and was extremely influential in elevating the artistic standards of ceramic production. The Sung era witnessed the rise of numerous regional kilns across the country, the famous wares of which are ranked among the most prized ceramics of modern day collections. The Chinese term tz'u, which is roughly translated into English as "porcelain," refers to glazed ceramics formed from ground petunse (porcelain stone) and/or kaolin clay and fired at high temperature. After firing, these ceramics develop a dense and impermeable body. The Sung dynasty saw substantial improvement in the quality of white porcelain and celadon, as well as the development of increasingly sophisticated techniques of mass production, which were practiced most famously at the Ting and Lung-ch'üan kilns. Some of the other best known high-quality wares of the era include those of the Kuan, Ju, Ko, and Chün kilns. The period also witnessed the beginnings of the ceramics industry at Ching-te-chen, Kiangsi. Although these kilns became the focal point for the production of underglaze blue porcelain in later periods, during the Sung they were best known for white and pale "shadow blue" ceramics. At the same time, the northern kilns at Tz'u-chou were producing lively black-and-white wares in folk style for popular consumption throughout the North. The era's most famous producers of black ceramics were, by contrast, the southern Chien kilns in Fukien and Chi-chou kilns in Kiangsi. When considering craftsmanship, it is clear that ceramic artistry reached unprecedented heights throughout many regions of Sung China.

Oval narcissus pot with light blue-green glaze

The ruins of the Ju kiln, located in the present-day confines of the Ch'ing-liang Temple in Pao-feng County, Honan, mark the site of one of the "five famous kilns" of the Sung dynasty. The specially commissioned Ju kiln, which produced the elegant pale celadon porcelain favored by the emperor Hui-tsung (r. 1101-1125), was patronized exclusively by the Sung imperial court. As a result, Ju ware is extremely rare and highly valued by collectors. In contrast to the extravagant and flamboyant glazes of T'ang dynasty ceramics, Sung wares generally appear monochrome and subdued. This oval-shaped bowl is evenly coated with a sky blue glaze, tending to pale green at the points of greater accumulation on the base, and light pink along the rim and edges. This exquisitely formed piece, with its smooth jade-like surface, is said to be the only known example of fully unadorned, crackle-less Ju ware.

Oval narcissus pot with light blue-green glaze, Ju ware, Sung dynasty

Kuan ware

Hibiscus shaped plate with light blue-green glaze

During the Sung dynasty, the official Kuan kilns produced wares that have come to be considered embodiments of the era's refined aesthetics. The Kuan kilns worked according to the specific needs of the imperial court, and were directly overseen by palace officials. The production of Kuan ware can be divided into Northern (960-1127) and Southern Sung (1127-1279) phases. Works from the first phase are also known as Pien-ching Kuan ware, after the capital of the Northern Sung. Wares of the second phase were fired at new kilns constructed after the court's evacuation of the North and reestablishment at Hangchow. During this second phase, the concentrated talent of the Kuan kilns focused on the production of ceramics for use by the imperial court. Transmitted examples of Kuan ware are extremely rare; those that do exist are characterized by stately, sturdy forms, somber glaze, and classical décor.

This hibiscus blossom shaped plate features a lovely blending of powder-green and pale blue glaze colors. During firing, the glaze shivered into a layered, irregular pattern of crackled lines. This crackle (or "crazing," as it is sometimes known), which is caused by the cooling differential between the glaze surface and the clay body underneath, gives the finished piece a soft, yet scintillating jade-like texture, refreshing visual quality, and classical elegance. Traditional Chinese connoisseurs often described Kuan ware as having, "purple rims and iron feet." The purplish color of the rim is caused by gravity, which pulls the glaze down from the rim during firing, leaving only a very thin coating that reveals the clay body underneath. The iron content of the clay gives it a purple tinge after firing, hence the "purple rims." The feet, which support the piece during firing, are left unglazed, and thus have the same iron-purple coloration.

Hibiscus shaped plate with light blue-green glaze, Kuan ware, Sung dynasty

Tea bowl with "hare's fur" striations on a black ground

Northern Sung scholars enjoyed drinking tea. To make the refined drink, partially fermented tea leaves were first pounded and packed into teacakes for preservation and storage. When brewing time came, these cakes were ground into powder and whisked with boiling water. This created a froth on the surface of the liquid, which Sung connoisseurs used as a standard for measuring the level of one's tea brewing capabilities. This tea bowl is coated with a thick layer of black glaze that completely covers its inside face and runs about halfway down its outer surface. Tiny pale brown impurities, pulled by the running glaze, create a pattern of threadlike needles on the vessel's surface. Sung literati described these striations as resembling a black rabbit's fur in autumn, hence the term "hare's fur." Court records from the reign of the emperor Hui-tsung allude to the presence of similarly decorated tea vessels in the Sung imperial court. This, combined with the discovery at the Chien kiln excavations in Fukien province of vessels bearing the inscriptions "for imperial use," and "a presented (to the court) tea vessel," demonstrates that the black-glazed tea wares of the Chien kilns were used by the Sung court.

Tea bowl with "hare's fur" striations on a black ground, Chien ware, Sung dynasty

Lung-ch'üan ware

Celadon bowl with lotus petal design

In China, the lotus is a symbol of gentility, and often used to decorate vessels and other objects. The surface of this bowl is incised with interconnecting petals and coated with a pale green glaze, so as to resemble a freshly blooming lotus. Holding the bowl is like holding a flower blossom; the natural experience of which inspired Sung artisans to create many types of foliated vessels in the shape of lotuses, chrysanthemums, sunflowers, and other blossoms. The glaze has a warm, soft, almost liquid quality that extends evenly across the surface of the bowl, running thin on the raised petals to reveal a hint of the grey body underneath. This effect gives the entire piece an aesthetically pleasing combination of balance and layered variation. Of all the glazes used by the Lung-ch'üan kilns, emerald-hinted celadon was the most critically acclaimed hue. During the Southern Sung, the Lung-ch'üan kilns, spurred by government and popular consumption, as well as an officially encouraged export trade, developed into a major center for ceramic production that extended across eight counties in modern Chekiang and down along the coast of Fukien. Famed for their finely-grained, durable greyish white bodies and thick, jade-like glaze, Lung-ch'üan wares were exported in large numbers to Korea, Japan, Okinawa, Southeast Asia, and even as far as the east coast of Africa.

Celadon bowl with lotus petal design, Lung-ch'üan ware, Sung dynasty

Ming Dynasty Ceramics

Around the beginning of the Ming dynasty in the mid-fourteenth century, the center of ceramic production shifted to the city of Ching-te-chen in Kiangsi. The imperial kilns at Ching-te-chen produced countless porcelain vessels for court consumption, each sealed with the reign mark of the emperor at the time. In addition to firing traditional celadon and other monochrome wares, the artisans at Ching-te-chen gradually developed a variety of new glazing techniques, including the partially exposed biscuit seen on some Yung-lo wares, Hsüan-te sacrificial red, Ch'eng-hua tou-ts'ai (contrasting colors), Hung-chih chiao-huang (winsome yellow), and Wan-li wu-ts'ai (five color).

Ming dynasty Yung-lo reign (1403-1424)
Vase with incised lotus design under sweet white glaze

The imperial court was extremely involved in porcelain production during the Yung-lo period. The popular "sweet white" glaze of the era, which was generated by raising the oxidation level during firing, was appreciated for its warm color and delicate translucence. Additional amounts of kaolin were added to the clay body, which increased the transparency of the final product and allowed for the high temperatures that were necessary for firing. With their extremely thin walls and refined glaze work, Yung-lo white porcelain was highly regarded by people of the Ming dynasty. This vase is decorated with a needle-fine incised pattern of interlocking floral scrolls, the soft and delicate lines of which have a very faint blue tinge. "Sweet white" perfectly captures the mood of this delicate, pure white piece.

Vase with incised lotus design under sweet white glaze, Yung-lo reign, Ming dynasty

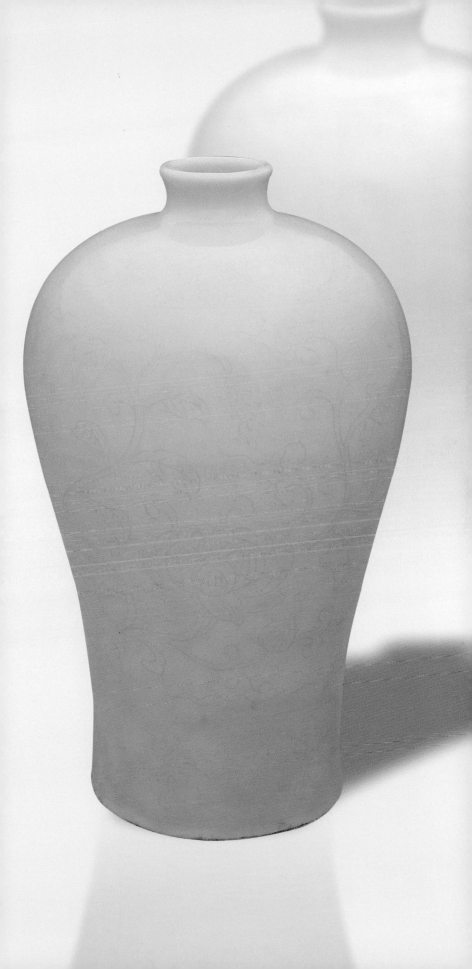

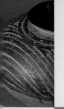

Hsüan-te reign (1426-1435)

Lamp with floral design in underglaze blue

Blue and white porcelain is characterized by the crisp, clear contrast achieved by painting blue cobalt pigment onto a pure white body. The shape of this lamp is based on that of the oil lamps commonly seen in the Middle East, while its surface is covered with complex lotus flower motifs and patterns derived from the decorative arts of India and Western Asia. By providing a venue for the expression of painterly skills, blue and white porcelain not only expresses the lyricism of Chinese ink painting, but also exhibits a visual showiness that captivates the viewers attention. Well received by Westerners, blue and white helped to expand the world market for Chinese porcelain. While this is a very small piece, it nevertheless reveals the essential qualities that turned Hsüan-te period porcelain into a world commodity.

Lamp with floral design in underglaze blue, Hsüan-te reign, Ming dynasty

Ch'eng-hua reign (1465-1487)

Chicken cups decorated in tou-ts'ai glaze

Porcelain glazing techniques improved dramatically during the Cheng-hua period. One particularly important innovation was the development of tou-ts'ai, which involves the combination of high-fired underglaze blue and low-fired overglaze enamels. Images are first outlined in cobalt blue, after which the entire piece is covered in a clear glaze and fired at high temperature. Once cooled, various brightly colored enamels are used to fill in the blue outlines. After this coloring process is completed, the piece is fired again, this time at a lower temperature, to set the enamels. The result is a visual contrast *tou* between the monchrome blue underglaze and the multi-colored overglaze colors *ts'ai*. This porcelain cup, decorated with small chickens, is a masterful example of tou-ts'ai glazing. The deep blue cobalt accentuates the pale red, yellow, brown, and green hues of the enamel that, both singly and in layered combination, create a visually stimulating and lively scene. The motifs within this scene act as auspicious emblems of familial harmony. Although the overall quality of porcelain craftsmanship declined after the Ch'eng-hua reign, the technological innovations and diverse decorative subject matter of the Ch'eng-hua era left much room for later creative endeavors, which continued until the collapse of the official kiln system in the Chung-chen reign (1628-1644). The technological and thematic creativity of these later periods laid a solid foundation for the glorious revival of Ching-te-chen under the Ch'ing emperors K'ang-hsi, Yung-cheng, and Ch'ien-lung.

Chicken cups decorated in tou-ts'ai glaze, Ch'eng-hua reign, Ming dynasty

Ming dynasty Ch'eng-te reign (1506-1521)

Flower receptacle with Indian lotus motif and Arabic inscription in blue underglaze

The sometimes greyish cobalt used during the reigns of the mid-Ming emperors Hung-chih and Ch'eng-te tended to be paler and more evenly applied than that of the preceeding reigns, lacking the expert brushwork effects seen on wares of the Hsüan-te and Ch'eng-hua reigns. The Ch'eng-te era saw the production of increasingly heavy porcelain pieces, many of which were intended for exhibition purposes. The spherical body of this vessel is topped with seven round holes used to hold flowers. The surface is decorated with a prayer written in Arabic, which may reflect Emperor Ch'eng-te's personal belief in Islam. It may also be the result of the strong economic trade and political ties that existed between Ming China and the Arabs of Central Asia, which fostered the spread of Islamic décor and vessel types into the porcelain workshops of Ching-te-chen.

Flower receptacle with Indian lotus motif and Arabic inscription in blue underglaze
Ch'eng-te reign, Ming dynasty

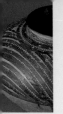

Ch'ing Dynasty Ceramics

During the early Ch'ing dynasty, the government reformed the administration of Ching-te-chen by terminating the previous pattern of sporadic eunuch oversight and appointing a series of specially selected officials specifically charged with the task of overseeing ceramic production. This new attention to administration was accompanied by a budgetary expansion that enabled the kilns to employ higher quality craftsmen and develop more detailed division of labor. The new degree of specialization and professionalism enabled by these reforms elevated the ceramic art of Ching-te-chen to an unprecedented level. The exquisite beauty of fen-ts'ai and fa-lang-ts'ai enameled porcelain is one of the hallmarks of this revival.

Ch'ing dynasty   K'ang-hsi ware

Tsun vase in the shape of a water chestnut with ruby red glaze

In addition to establishing official kilns at Ching-te-chen, the government under the K'ang-hsi emperor also instituted a policy of commissioning large numbers of imperial wares from private kilns. This practice spurred the development of the region's popular ceramic industry. In its earliest incarnation, the term *tsun* refered to a type of round-footed ritual bronze wine vessel used commonly in ancient China. With the rise of antiquarianism in the Sung dynasty, potters began producing ceramic imitations of these vessels, which were used, not as wine containers, but rather as flower vases. The long neck, flat shoulders, and rounded belly of this vessel gives it the semblance of an oversized water chestnut. Copper, the element responsible for the ruby red color of the glaze, is a notoriously unstable ingredient, easily influenced by the shifting temperatures of the kiln. Thus, the deep, richly textured quality of this vessel's glaze is a particularly noteworthy achievement.

Tsun vase in the shape of a water chestnut with ruby red glaze, K'ang-hsi ware, Ch'ing dynasty

Teapot with landscape scene in blue enamel among mille-fleur ground

Fa-lang-ts'ai, which refers to porcelain painted with enamel colors, are among the most prized of all ceramics. The use of fa-lang enameling, a technique imported from the West, began during the reign of the K'ang-hsi emperor (r. 1662-1722) with the production of copper bodied enamelware. In the year 1727, the technique was first applied to porcelain. The versatility of fa-lang enamels allowed Chinese craftsmen to achieve a wide variety of pictographic effects, ranging from birds and flowers to landscapes and human subjects. Emperor Yung-cheng was deeply concerned with the production of porcelain, and appointed several supervisors to oversee production at the Ching-te-chen kilns. One of these officials was T'ang Ying, an accomplished artisan in his own right, who personally researched ceramic techniques and developed some seventy-five new glazes. Under his direction, the imperial kilns produced both fine imitations of classical wares and creative new designs. The lid and body of this teapot are both covered with floral décor. Delicate lines of blue glaze form a detailed rendition of a Chinese landscape painting, with mountains, houses, streams, bridges, and even a calligraphic inscription. Judging from the quality of this piece, it is likely that it was produced by masters from the imperial kiln.

Teapot with landscape scene in blue enamel among mille-fleur ground
Yung-cheng ware, Ch'ing dynasty

Chinese Cloisonné

Enamelware, known in Chinese as *fa-lang*, after the Ming dynasty term for the Eastern Mediterranean region from where these objects were first imported, is produced by fusing glass-based glaze onto a metallic surface. Enamelware is generally divided into three categories: cloisonné, where the enamel is fused within wire cells; champlevé, where enamel is fused into hollowed-out grooves; and painted enamel, where the design is painted onto a plain surface.

Cloisonné box with lotus-spray design, Ching-tai reign, Ming dynasty

Ching-t'ai reign (1506-1521)

Cloisonné box with lotus-spray design

Although cloisonné enamelling techniques were first introduced to China by Arabian craftsmen in Yüan dynasty, the Ching-t'ai reign of the Ming dynasty marks the artistic pinnacle of Chinese cloisonné.

This bronze cloisonné box is adorned with a lively design of colorful lotus flowers in high relief. Similar motifs can be found on early Ming porcelain. A pale blue glaze fills the background of the lid and body, and the gilded interior of the box bears the inscription: "Made in the Reign of the Great Ming Emperor Ching-t'ai."

Ch'ing dynasty K'ang-hsi reign (1622-1722)

Painted enamel plate with phoenix decoration

The decoration of painted enamelware often resembles that of porcelain, and for this reason, painted enamelware was once popularly known as "foreign porcelain." Painted enamel is usually applied to a metal base,

but other materials are sometimes used as well.

Painted enamelware was first imported to China in the Ch'ing dynasty. Enthralled by these wares, the emperor K'ang-hsi ordered the master artisans in his employ to study and master the technique. The introduction of this innovative approach to enamelling brought a new vibrancy to the art that enabled it to surpass the accomplishments of the Ming. Thus, the reigns of the K'ang-hsi, Yung-cheng, and Ch'ien-lung emperors, which span the second half of the seventeenth and entire eighteenth century, constitute the second golden age of Chinese enamelware.

This bronze plate is adorned with sixteen petals surrounded by phoenix motifs. The flat, broad rim is encircled with pale blue floral scrolls. The inner base is filled with the image of eight soaring phoenixes with centrally converging tails. The inscription, "Imperially Produced in the Reign of K'ang-hsi," written in standard script, can be found at the center of the plate's underside.

Painted enamel plate with phoenix decoration, K'ang-hsi reign, Ch'ing dynasty

Ten enameled glass snuff bottles

Snuff is created from ground tobacco, generally combined with different herbal ingredients that give it a variety of colors and scents. In early days, people believed that the gentle inhalation of snuff could cure headaches, colds, and congestion. Records suggest that snuff was first brought to China from Italy in the early 1580s. By the seventeenth century, its use was widespread. During the Ch'ing dynasty, snuff became a popular alternative to smoking tobacco, which was prohibited by the new Manchu imperial house. However, the indulgers in this new habit soon found imported European snuffboxes unsuitable for storing the substance in the humid Chinese climate. An answer was found by domestic artisans, who quickly developed a new industry—snuff bottles.

During the Ch'ing dynasty, the use of snuff prevailed at all levels of society, from the emperor and imperial court to rural peasants in remote districts. The imperial palace employed special craftsmen to create snuff bottles out of various precious materials for the emperor's amusement. Snuff bottles were also occasionally commissioned from private workshops and received as diplomatic gifts from Western envoys.

The production of snuff bottles peaked during the reign of Emperor Ch'ien-lung. The frequent exchange of these bottles between high-ranking nobles and officials gave them a certain cache that inspired high prices and feverish collection. Bottles were crafted in a variety of shapes from many different materials, including porcelain, agate, glass, jade, crystal, wood, ivory, and bamboo. Yet the greatest praise was reserved for painted enamel bottles, which were often further embellished with exquisite gold, bronze, glass, porcelain décor. These ten bottles feature landscapes, portraits, flowers, and other decorative illustrations. Their fine quality suggests that they were made by master craftsmen.

Set of ten painted enamel glass snuff bottles, Ch'ing dynasty

Jade

In China, "jade" historically referred to any beautiful stone. Jade carvings are an important component of the Chinese artistic tradition, with their own enduring history and unique characteristics.

Many ancient jade pieces were ritual artifacts used in ceremonies dedicated to the spirit world. Jade *pi* discs and *ts'ung* tubes, representing the connection of heaven with earth and the bond between people and spirits, were especially numerous. Under the influence of Confucianism during the Eastern Chou dynasty, jade came to symbolize the moral ruler, and jade carvings became a popular bodily adornment. Jade was also thought to prevent the physical decay of the dead and facilitate rebirth, and was often buried with the deceased. This use of jade in funeral rites contributed to its broad mystical significance. Jade was also crafted into such ornaments as combs, hairpins, rings, bracelets, decorative pins, and pendants. Canes, belts, and hats were also often inlaid or decorated with jade.

The importance of jade art has extended to the present: shopping for jade, wearing jade, and giving jade as a gift are all common practices in contemporary society. Whether declaring one's commitment to a loved one or congratulating one's child on his or her marriage, jade is always the perfect gift. Not only does jade make a beautiful adornment, but Chinese people also believe that it gives protection from evil, wards off calamity, and brings luck to the bearer.

Jade kuei tablet with mythical bird design

Jade *kuei*, ceremonial pieces with a broad base and narrow top, probably developed from stone-age tools such as knives and axes. This kuei is decorated on both sides: one side bears an eagle design while the other has a bird-head pattern. The ancient inhabitants of the modern-day coastal provinces of Liaotung, Shantung, Chekiang, and Kiangsu believed that the High God gave life to their ancestors by way of mythical bird intermediaries. Therefore, they incised their kuei tablets, symbols of rank and status, with supernatural bird images. The Ch'ing dynasty emperor Ch'ien-lung treasured this particular kuei, and ordered it to be engraved with his poetry and official seal. He also had it mounted upright on a wooden stand. To make out the images properly, the kuei should be viewed from the bottom up, as it was placed upside down when given their wooden stands.

Above: Jade ts'ung, Liang-chu culture, Neolithic period
Right: Jade kuei tablet with mythical bird design, Neolithic period

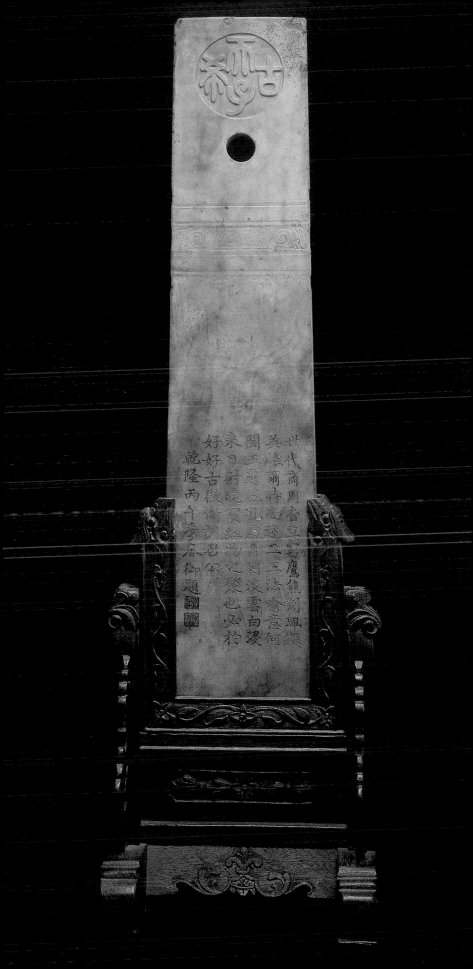

世代商周尊斝鷹熊刻珮擬
英端爾時鬲逑二王法喻意何
開匜覆風孔廉月圓浪雲白漫
來日射曉震紅拋之聚也必祊
好古徵訓巳公
乾隆丙午季春御題

Han dynasty

Jade pig wrapped in gold leaf

There is a Chinese saying that goes, "Jade concentrates in the mountains and rivers." The Chinese have long thought that jade embodies the patterns of nature, and they have carved jade into intricate patterns and imbued it with various meanings. Because the ancient Chinese believed that jade could keep the body from decaying, and cause the dead to live again, they buried jade along with the deceased. Jade cicadas were often placed in the mouths of the dead, while jade pigs were placed in their hands. The small, cylindrically-shaped pig seen here can be easily grasped in the hand, and is decorated with a simply carved mouth, nose, and eyes. Pigs were probably the first animals domesticated in ancient China. Grasped in the hand, they are thus both a symbol of plentitude and an indication of the ancient transition from a hunting and fishing economy to a society focused around sedentary, agricultural activity.

Grasping a jade pig is thus both a literal and symbolic means of holding onto one's wealth after death—all the more so when the value of the pig is further enhanced by its gold covering.

Jade pig wrapped in gold leaf, Han dynasty

Ming dynasty

Jade vase in the shape of a carp

Ming dynasty literati had sophisticated taste, and the decorations and implements found in the literati study were highly refined and finely crafted. To satisfy these tastes, jade craftsmen produced a large variety of studio tools and decorations, such as brush holders, paperweights, water droppers, and inkstones. The jade flower vase seen here is carved in the

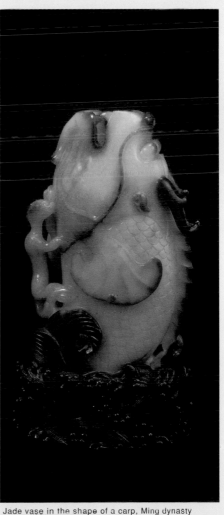

likeness of a leaping carp swimming upstream. A small dragon is carved on the carp's belly. The Chinese have a saying that goes, "A carp leaps through the Dragon Gate," which is used to describe a scholar who succeeds in the civil service examinations. This saying refers to the swiftly flowing waters around a section of the Yellow River known as the Dragon Gate, where carp have to swim against the current and leap through the rapids. Only a few ever complete the journey through the rapids, and those who do are said to turn into dragons, while those who do not remain simple fish. This is why the Chinese also have the saying, "Once past the Dragon Gate, one's value increases a hundred-fold," which is a poetic way of describing a person who strives for great accomplishment and finally achieves fame and success. Referring to the fish that leaps through the Dragon Gate and becomes a dragon is also a way of congratulating someone and wishing them good fortune. With its elongated head and newly grown feet, this jade carp is clearly on the verge of becoming a dragon. Aside from serving as a flower vase, the piece is exquisitely carved, and expresses a striving for well-being and beauty. It is a fitting representative of the level that the art of jade carving had attained by the Ming and Ch'ing dynasties.

Jade vase in the shape of a carp, Ming dynasty

Jade Cabbage

The Jade Cabbage is one of the National Palace Museum's star pieces, and always attracts attention. Its fame lies in the rare delicacy with which it combines the natural beauty of jade with a consummate carving style. The jade used for this piece is found in regions of China's Yunnan Province and Myanmar. This type of jade is at times greenish (*ts'ui*), and at times reddish (*fei*) in color, and is thus generally referred to in Chinese as *ts'ui-fei* or, in English, as "jadeite." It belongs to the class of hard jade, which differs from the softer nephrite jade traditionally used in Chinese art.

The white part of the jade forms the stem of the cabbage, while the seemingly natural curls of the blue-green portion represent the plant's leaves. With its clearly carved fibers and veins, this piece is exceptionally lifelike, showing great ingenuity in planning and execution. The insects that crawl along the cabbage leaves—a katydid and a grasshopper—are known to breed in great numbers, and so have come to symbolize fertility. For instance, the ode *Katydid* in the classic *Book of Poetry* (*Shih ching*) is a piece that congratulates its addressee on his many sons and grandsons.

This piece was originally displayed in the Palace of Eternal Harmony (*Yung-ho kung*) in Peking's Forbidden City. During the final years of the Ch'ing dynasty, the imperial concubine Ching Fei resided in this palace. The cabbage may have been part of her dowry. Aside from symbolizing the purity of the bride, the piece wishes the new couple plentiful sons and grandsons and thus an unbroken dynastic line stretching into the distant future.

Jade Cabbage, Ch'ing dynasty

Hindustan

Green jade flower-shaped bowl with gold inlay

Hindustan refers to the North Indian and Mongolian plateau region at the far western extremity of the Ch'ing empire. With rich and varied materials producing fine, delicate patterns, the arts of this region used gold, silver, and colorful stone or glass inlay to create magnificent jade pieces. The style of these pieces differs substantially from the simple and unadorned elegance of traditional Chinese jade craft. After the Ch'ien-lung Emperor pacified the Sinkiang region in the mid-eighteenth century, these jade pieces, with their deeply exotic, Islamic flavor, were brought to China in large numbers. They numbered among the emperor's favorite treasures.

As this piece suggests, Hindustan jades mostly took the form of thin, delicate bowls, ladles, plates, and boxes, with traced floral decorations on their exterior. Many were inlaid with gold and silver thread, colored stones, and glass. The style of these foreign wares had a strong influence on the arts of China.

Meat-shaped stone

The Meat-shaped Stone ranks with the Jade Cabbage as one of the Museum's most famous, and most ingenious, pieces. We viewers know perfectly well that this is just a cold, hard piece of stone. Yet it so closely resembles a tender, juicy piece of Tung-p'o style pork that our mouths water at the sight, and we have to ask ourselves whether this in fact a natural stone or some kind of artificial construction.

This piece is crafted from an opaque kind of layered rock whose veins accrue layer upon layer. Recognizing this special quality, the artisan skillfully enhanced the stone by boring small holes into its surface. This not only produced the dimpled effect of hair follicles, but also differentiated the surface, allowing dye to adhere more readily to the stone. The next step involved the application of a brownish-red color to the top dimpled layer, giving the rock the appearance of a soy-soaked piece of meat.

The traditional Chinese notion of "ingenious carving" refers to a crafting process that follows the natural shape, lines, and coloring of the stone. This type of carving, in which the individual expresses his or her creativity within externally imposed limits, aspires to reconcile the natural with the artificial. This piece is an irreproducible treasure that exemplifies this approach to carving.

Above: Meat-shaped Stone, Ch'ing dynasty
Left: Green jade flower-shaped bowl with gold inlay, Hindustan, Ch'ing dynasty

Studio Items and Carvings

The Ch'ing court established various workshops to create works of art specifically for imperial consumption. Court patronage led to rapid improvement in the standards of many tradition crafts, as well as a penchant for delicacy and miniatures, as seen in the fine detail of the era's lacquerware and bamboo, ivory, and nutshell carving. Some of these objects were produced by private craftsmen, while others were created by artisans in the imperial ateliers.

Lacquerware

Modern archaeological discoveries show that people of the ancient Ho-mu-tu culture, located in present day Chekiang, began applying the sap of lacquer trees to objects as early as 5000 B.C. Over the subsequent millennia, the art of Chinese lacquering evolved from early monochrome painting into a rich craft with great array of inlay, painting, incising, and carving techniques. Carved lacquerware can be further subdivided into several categories of so-called t'i-hsi lacquer, which features multiple layers of different color, as well as objects decorated in monochrome, most commonly red, yellow, and black.

Ming dynasty Yung-lo reign
Carved red lacquer vase with floral motif

Artists create this type of lacquerware by carving into pre-applied layers of lacquer on the vessel's surface. The technique requires skill and patience, for it is difficult to attain the desired degree of hardness, as lacquer is a naturally soft material and many layers are required to create the desired surface quality. Therefore, a time consuming process of layering, with sufficient time allotted for each layer to dry, is necessary before carving can finally begin. Sometimes hundreds of layers are needed to create the desired surface. This technique originated in the T'ang dynasty and slowly matured in the Sung and Yüan. Under the encouragement and support of the early Ming emperor Yung-lo, the art of lacquer carving was integrated into the palace workshop system, giving it a new degree of discipline and specialization. The carved lacquerware of the Yung-lo era thus represents one of the greatest accomplishments of Ming and Ch'ing dynasty artisans. The body of this carved red lacquer vase is covered with a dense floral motif called the "Four Seasons Flower." The form of the vase is delicate and natural, while the carving is round and balanced. The bottom and interior of the vase are painted with monochrome black lacquer, and the bottom bears the needle-carved inscription "Produced in the Reign of Great Ming Emperor Yung-lo."

Carved red lacquer vase with floral motif, Yung-lo reign, Ming dynasty

Gold-etched painted lacquer chest with dragon and phoenix motifs

Gold-etching is a special technique that involves the incision of fine patterns on the surface of a lacquered vessel with a needle or thin knife. These grooves are next filled, first with a different colored lacquer, and then with a layer of gold. The final result is a scintillating golden design. The same technique was also used with silver. This lacquer chest contains some forty-three snuff bottles, walnut carvings, and other miniature curios.

Above: Peony shaped carved black lacquer plate with twin phoenix décor, Yüan dynasty

Below: Circular box with peony design in mother-of-pearl inlay, Ming dynasty

Right: Gold-etched painted lacquer chest with dragon and phoenix motifs, Ch'ing dynasty

Bamboo Carving

Bamboo serves a wide variety of functions, and can be used to craft furniture, buildings, and household goods. Traditional Chinese scholars often regarded its graceful, natural form as a symbol of purity and dignity. It has long been a popular subject for Chinese painters and a medium used by Chinese carvers and other craftsmen.

Ming dynasty Chu San-sung
Carved bamboo brush holder

High relief carving was used to create the image of a woman on this brush holder, which closely resembles that found in a wood block printed edition, illustrated by the Ming painter Ch'en Hung-shou, of the *Romance of the Western Chamber*. A famous Chinese play, the *Romance* tells the story of two star-crossed lovers who strive to stay together despite the objections of their families. Their romance is sustained with the help of a maid, who acts as an intermediary, delivering messages and love letters between them and helping to arrange secret meetings. The scene depicted in this illustration is that of the heroine, Ts'ui Ying-ying, demurely reading letters from her lover, while the maid hides behind a screen, secretly observing her mistress's reaction. During the latter half of the Ming dynasty, Chia-ting (part of present day

Carved bamboo brush holder, Chu San-sung, Ming dynasty

Shanghai) and Chin-ling (present day Nanking) became the centers of the bamboo carving industry. "The Three Chu's of Chiating," Chu Ho, Chu Ying, and Chu Chih-cheng, were three successive generations of a famous family of bamboo artists. This brush holder is attributed to Chu Chih-cheng on the basis of the inscription San-sung (Chih-cheng's moniker) found on the lower right-hand corner of the screen.

Carved bamboo armrest

Armrests such as this were used by scholars when writing calligraphy.

Carved bamboo armrest, Ch'ing dynasty

Carved boxwood lohan scratching back

Boxwood is an excellent material for woodcarving, famous for its delicate grain and graceful color. In this boxwood carving, an anonymous craftsman captures the satisfied expression of a lohan scratching his back. Lohan, known as arhats in Indian Buddhism, are monks who have achieved enlightenment. This lohan sits cross-legged, wrapped in his monk robes. His back is bared, allowing him to fully experience the pleasures of scratching. Although the figure is no taller than two inches in height, it is carved with exquisite detail and is highly naturalistic. The left leg of the lohan, with its accurate muscle and bone structure, offers a clear example of this attention to realism. The inclusion of a dog roaming in the foreground, examining the lohan, adds an everyday quality to the scene.

Carved boxwood lohan scratching back, Middle to late Ch'ing dynasty

Chen Tsu-chang

Miniature boat carved from an olive pit

Chen Tsu-chang was a famous craftsman of the Ch'ing imperial court best known for ivory carving. He did, however, also carve fruit pits and nutshells. Here, the artist uses the

Miniature boat carved from an olive pit, Chen Tsu-chang, Ch'ing dynasty

natural shape of the olive pit to craft a miniature boat, which measures only one and a half inches in length. The boat contains tiny figures, as well as

chairs, tables, plates, and cups. The windows and doors can be opened and shut, and the bottom of the boat bears the famous *Latter Ode on the Red Cliff* by the Sung dynasty poet and statesman Su Tung-p'o. All three hundred characters of the ode are included, as well as a dated signature by the craftsmen. This boat represents the technical pinnacle of Chinese fruit pit and shell carving.

Bamboo curio cabinet

This curio cabinet is intricately and ingeniously designed. When closed, it is oval in shape, but when opened, the inner layers can be reassembled to form a miniature screen. Turned around, the piece becomes a display cabinet. The outside is wrapped in thin strips of bamboo, and decorated with flowers and other intricate designs. The box has spaces for twenty-seven objects, and includes a secret drawer in the bottom for a painting or calligraphy handscroll. The curio cabinets in the National Palace Museum were once known as "Hundred Treasure Chests," used by collectors to hold various precious objects. Imperial chests were more delicately designed than most, as many of the treasures were particularly small, and their compartments were specifically customized to the size and shape of the objects placed within.

Bamboo curio cabinet, Ch'ing dynasty

Bone Carvings

The carving of bone began in China during Neolithic times. From the beginning, the favored material of bone carvers was ivory, with its naturally smooth and lustrous texture. According to archaeological research, herds of elephants used to live in the vicinity of the Yellow River, but as time passed, pachyderms slowly disappeared from the region. Nevertheless, ivory production and carving continued to flourish in China, becoming especially popular in the Ming and Ch'ing dynasties.

Ch'ing dynasty

Ivory food container

This ivory carved box, so delicate that parts of it resemble a silk tapestry, is exquisitely adorned with human figures, animals, birds, trees, architecture, and boats. Beneath this scene is a pattern of vertical lines, which have been hollowed out to form identical rows. The eight ribbon motifs and handle have been dyed with light blue and red, colors that contrast beautifully with the milky white ivory. On the handle are carvings of the auspicious Eight Immortals, which bring life to the entire piece. Although this ornate layered box was in all likelihood not actually used to store food, its shape corresponds to food containers typical of the period.

The immense popularity of ivory carving in China during the sixteenth, seventeenth, and eight-eenth centuries led to the importation of large quantities of ivory from Africa. This box was carved using African ivory.

Above: Carved ivory landscape scene, Ch'ien-lung reign, Ch'ing dynasty
Right: Ivory food container, Ch'ing dynasty

The Four Treasures of the Scholar's Study

The "Four Treasures" of the scholar's study—brush, ink, paper, and inkstone—are used to create Chinese calligraphy and painting. Brushes were used for writing as early as the Neolithic. By the third century B.C., the use of writing brushes was widespread, facilitating the development of Chinese calligraphy and painting. Ink is produced from charcoal, most commonly derived from pine and paulownia wood. Paper, created with plant fibers, is the most common medium for Chinese painting and calligraphy. When watered down ink touches the paper, it diffuses quickly, instilling a sense of spontaneity and natural randomness. Inkstones are crafted from specially selected and processed natural stones. These four treasures are all products of nature—animal fur, trunks of bamboo, burnt plant fibers, and water worn rocks. They are at once tools and artistic objects—the inkstones of famous calligraphers, the paper of the Southern T'ang palaces, the ink of the imperial ateliers—all are priceless artifacts.

Ming dynasty Ch'eng Chün-fang

Ink stick with inscription *K'un-lun t'ien chu* (Heavenly Pillar of Mt. K'un-lun)

The quality of ink is a determining factor of artistic achievement. The primary attributes used to rank the quality of an inkstick are solidity, viscosity, odor, and color. During the T'ang and Sung dynasties, the appreciation of ink, like the connoisseurship of tea, became a popular literati pastime. Surviving poems and other writing even attest to personal friendships between ink makers and many of the era's leading scholar-officials. The spread of literacy in the late Ming led to a surge in

the value of ink, which in turn spurred competition between ink craftsmen. Such competition inspired a new attention to quality, as well as the introduction of many innovative, eye-catching ink stick shapes and decorative motifs.

The famous and highly regarded Ming dynasty ink craftsman and scholar, Chiao Hung, once wrote ten odes on ink for Ch'eng Chün-fang. Ch'eng's workshop sculpted these odes into their inksticks. The present inkstick bears an illustration that closely resembles a wood block print found in the *Ch'eng-shih mo-y'an* (*Collection of Ch'eng Ink Rubbings*), and is thus an excellent example of fine Ming dynasty ink. Ch'eng, a native of Anhui, was both a skilled craftsman and collector of ink. One of his inkstick designs, produced by a workshop known as the *Pao-mo chai* (Precious Ink Studio), was even presented to the imperial court. The *Ch'eng-shih mo-y'an*, published in 1605, is Ch'eng's compilation of 519 different inkstick designs. The text was highly regarded and used by literati-scholars throughout China.

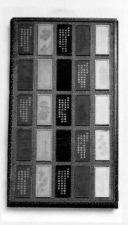

Above right: Brush cases with cloud and dragon design in colored lacquer,
Chia-ching reign (1522-1566), Ming dynasty
Above left: Tuan inkstone, Sung dynasty
Below right: Multicolored ink stick with imperial poems, Ch'ing dynasty
Below left: Ink stick with inscription *K'un-lun t'ien chu* (Heavenly Pillar of Mt. K'un-lun)
Ch'eng Chün-fang, Ming dynasty

Religious Artifacts

Religious faith is one of the pillars of the human spirit, and religious artifacts are not only objects of aesthetic beauty, but also a means of spreading religious messages. These beautiful and mysterious works enable the faithful to experience the aesthetic expression of religious emotion. The National Palace Musuem's collection of Buddhist relics includes objects crafted both in Tibet and China. The relics are divided into three major categories: sutras, statuary, and religious vessels. There are many pieces to enjoy in this elegant and moving collection.

Northern Wei dynasty

Seated image of Sakyamuni Buddha

Buddhism spread throughout China during the period of the so-called Northern and Southern dynasties (essentially the fourth to sixth centuries A.D.). The widespread popularity of the faith led to the large-scale creation of Buddhist images. This gilded bronze statue of the Buddha from the Northern Wei period (386-534) is delicately and intricately formed. Many gilded bronze statues were small in size, allowing for easy transport. They served as auspicious traveling relics, but could also be used for personal worship in the home.

This figure and platform were cast as a single piece, with the large halo, or mandorla, attached in a second casting. The fiery motifs that encircle the halo reflect and enhance the power of the image. The illustration on the back can be divided into three sections. In the top register, two Buddhas sit side by side, flanked by images of Vimalakirti and Manjusri in conversation. The middle register shows the Buddha preaching in Deer Park, while the lower register depicts the story of the Buddha's birth. The structure and sequence of the illustrations are orderly and carefully planned, and the final image represents a classic example of Northern Wei Tai-ho period (fifth century A.D.) Buddhist statuary.

Seated image of Sakyamuni Buddha, Northern Wei dynasty

Ch'ien-lung reign

Skull offering bowl

The Tibetan attitude towards death differs vastly from that of the Chinese. The deceased are honored with a "Heavenly Funeral," in which their bodies are returned to nature. Tibetans believe that the merit accumulated during a monk's life is preserved in his bones, which are thus believed to have auspicious, magical power. In the past, it was even believed that religious texts would appear on the bones of the holiest monks. Thus, the bones of lamas were carved to craft ritual vessels, rosaries, hand-drums, and offering bowls. The uniquely Tibetan quality of this skull offering bowl is further emphasized by its brightly colored adornment.

Skull offering bowl, Ch'ien-lung reign, Ch'ing dynasty

Ch'ien-lung reign

Tsongkhapa

Tsongkhapa was a major Buddhist reformer and the founder of the Yellow Hat sect of Tibetan Buddhism. This cast gold statue depicts Tsongkhapa with his hands held in the preaching mudra. Lilies sprout from his palms, and in the top of the lilies rest a religious text and sword, both symbols of wisdom. Iconographically speaking, such symbolism implies that Tsongkhapa was a reincarnation of Manjusri, the Boddhisattva of Wisdom. The inscriptions on the back, in Chinese, Manchurian, Mongolian, and Tibetan, reveal that the statue was commissioned by Emperor Ch'ien-lung. The high arching nose and simple flowing drapery are typical of Tibetan casting style, while the wide back, solid lower body and shiny metallic color are characteristics of Ch'ing imperial craftsmanship.

Ch'ing dynasty Ch'ien-lung reign

Right-spiraling conch

The conch is a highly symbolic and important Buddhist ritual implement. It serves as both a horn and holy water container, as well as being an important symbol of reincarnation. Most conches grow in a left-spiraling direction, and right-spiraling examples are extremely rare. Tibetan Buddhists treasured such conches as powerful magical objects. During the Ch'ing dynasty, the conch was believed to have the power to calm the seas, and was placed aboard naval vessels as a protective talisman. This conch has a special historical connection with Taiwan, as it was carried to Taiwan in 1788 by the naval fleet of General Fu K'ang-an, on a mission to quell a Taiwanese rebellion.

Above: Right-spiraling conch, Ch'ien-lung reign, Ch'ing dynasty
Below: Tsongkhapa, Ch'ien-lung reign, Ch'ing dynasty

Rare Books and Documents

The Museum's collection of books and documents, which includes rare early printed editions, Manchu and Mongolian texts, and a variety of important archival records, numbers approximately 570,000 items.

Complete Collection of the Four Treasuries

Since the beginning of Chinese imperial history, many great efforts have been made to gather and compile literary documents. The seminal Ch'ing dynasty work, *Complete Collection of the Four Treasuries*, was a continuation and extension of this tradition. *The Treasuries* include around 3400 of the most important classical texts, spanning a total of over 36,000 volumes. The contents of the collection are divided into four major categories: classics, histories, biographies, and literary works. The directors of the project spent years selecting and cross-checking the collection's contents. The result of their massive effort was the most comprehensive and academically credible collection to date. Ch'ien-lung initiated the project in the thirty-seventh year of his reign (1772) with a decree commanding each of the empire's provinces to gather and submit books to the court. After fifteen years and the diligent efforts of some 3800 scholars, the masterpiece was finished. A total of seven hand-written copies of the entire compilation were produced and distributed to the Forbidden City, the Imperial Palace at Shenyang, Ch'ien-lung's summer palace at Rehol, the emperor's summer palace in Peking (Yüan-ming-yüan), and centers of learning in Chenkiang, Yangchow, and Hangchow. However, the wars and natural disasters of the intervening two centuries caused the destruction or damage of five of these copies. Fortunately, the edition now in the National Palace Museum, originally kept in the Forbidden City, was the first and finest of these copies. In total, it numbers 36,381 volumes, containing 3471 individual texts divided into over 79,300 chapters.

Left first: Envoy's account of Korea (printed edition), Hsüan-ho reign (1119-1125), Sung dynasty
Left second: Yung-lo ta-tien (Vast Documents of the Yung-lo Era), Ming dynasty
Left third: Diaries of Rest and Repose, Ch'ing dynasty
Left fourth: Complete Collection of the Four Treasuries, Ch'ing dynasty
Offset: Collection of State Correspondence, Ch'ing dynasty

Silk Tapestry and Embroidery

China has, for millennia, been known throughout the world as a producer of fine silk. Her most famous textiles are silk tapestry and embroidery. The distinguishing feature of silk tapestry (or k'o-ssu "cut silk" in Chinese) is the use of discontinuous horizontal (weft) threads instead of threads that run the whole width of the fabric, as they do in ordinary woven silks. In silk tapestry, the weft is introduced only at the point where its particular color is required in the design. The shuttle carries the colored weft back and forth within a predetermined pattern until the design is complete. When the completed tapestry is held up to the light, the tooth-like gaps between different weft patterns look the lines of a carving knife, hence the term "cut silk."

Embroidery refers to any kind of needlework applied to woven silk, twill, damask, brocade, or other fabric. Early embroidery was used as decoration on clothing and other objects of everyday use. Around the start of the second millennium A.D., the increased appreciation of calligraphy and paintings led to the adoption of embroidery for creating copies of paintings and illustrations. The process of producing silk tapestry and embroidery is painstakingly difficult, requiring substantial skill and patience. The textile collection of the National Palace Museum consists primarily of pieces that are designed and mounted in the manner of paintings and calligraphy. The ease with which these works are mistaken for actual painting and calligraphy demonstrates their masterful quality.

Above: Silk tapestry, Chu K'o-jo, Sung dynasty
Right: Cassia's Heavenly Fragrance, Ku Hsiu,
Ch'ing dynasty

Ch'ing Court Jewelry and Personal Ornaments

The Museum's collection of clothing and jewelry consists primarily of Ch'ing dynasty court attire; some examples include crowns, hairpins, and belts. Many of these objects were designed according to traditional Chinese models, while others are infused with ethnic Manchurian styles. According to historical records, Ch'ing imperial attire was dictated by strict rules and regulations. Not only was there a distinction between summer and winter clothing, but also rules for formal, casual, courtly, and ritual wear. Hats and decorative accessories, such as necklaces and bracelets, were also strictly regulated.

Above: Imperial consort summer hat
Right: *Shuang-hsi* (double happiness) crown, Ch'ing dynasty

Shuang-hsi (double happiness) crown

This Shuang-hsi crown is commonly called a *t'ien-tzu*. T'ien-tzu were worn by Manchurian women in combination with designated clothing during special important festivals or days of religious significance. The crowns are usually decorated with precious materials such as gold, jade, beads, agate, amber, and pearls.

Worth noting are the feathers, which come from a precious green-colored bird, and are used to form the twin *hsi* characters. The feathers also make up the leaves and other brightly colored green areas. This brilliant shade of green has a dazzling effect when coupled with the red coral, green jade, and white pearls which adorn the crown.

Orientation

Address: 221 Chih-shan Rd., Sec. 2, Wai-shuang-hsi Taipei, 111 Taiwan, R.O.C.

Telephone: (886-2) 2881-2021   Fax: (886-2) 2882-1440

Web: http://www.npm.gov.tw

Main Building

Hours

Open daily from 9 a.m. to 5 p.m.

Admission

Standard: NT$100

Group Ticket: NT$80 per person (minimum 20 people)

Discount: NT$50 (available to R.O.C. military, police, and students, as well as international students with student ID)

Free Admission

Children under 110 cm and seniors over 65; retired military, civil servants, and teachers; mentally or physically handicapped visitors, together with one companion; military, police, and student groups (requires advance application); university-level students and teachers in art-related fields with NPM visitor passes; visitors with Bureau of Tourism passes; visitors with Council on Museum Studies member badges.

Guided Tours

Free, regularly scheduled tours are provided in Mandarin, Taiwanese, and English. Please register in advance at the Information Desk and return again to the desk shortly before the scheduled tour. Tour times are as follows:

＊Mandarin: Daily at 9:30 a.m and 2:30 p.m.

＊English: Daily at 10:00 a.m. and 3:00 p.m.

＊Special Topics (Mandarin): Daily at 10:00 a.m. and 3:30 p.m.

Audio Guide

The audio tour desk (ext. 524), located just inside the main entrance on the first floor, has Mandarin, English, and Japanese language tours available for rent.

Handicapped Services

＊Wheelchairs are available from the checkroom counter on the first floor.

＊Wheelchair-accessible restrooms are located by the east elevators.

Gift Shops

Gift shops are located in the basement and on the first floor.

Refreshments

＊Museum Restaurant: Located outside and to the west of the main building. Open daily from 9 a.m. to 9 p.m. Offers simple meals, Chinese dishes, and hot and cold beverages.

＊San Hsi T'ang Tea Room: Enjoy a wide selection of teas and Chinese snacks in this traditional Chinese-style tea room on the fourth floor of the main building.

＊East Wing Pavilion: Offers hot and cold beverages and snacks. Located in the east wing, on the fourth floor of the main building.

Library (2nd, 3rd, and 4th floors of the Library Building)

Open daily Monday to Saturday from 9 a.m. to 5 p.m. Closed Sundays and national holidays.Admission cards are available free to anyone over the age of 16. To apply, please bring identification and two passport sized photos to the library service desk.

Chih-shan Garden

Open daily Tuesday to Sunday from 7 a.m. to 7 p.m. Closed Mondays.

Admission: NT$10

Snack Shop. Located to the left of the entrance to the museum driveway. Offers hot and cold beverages, Taiwanese specialties, and a wide selection of snacks.

Chih-te Garden

Hours: No restrictions on entry.

Admission: Free

Chang Dai-ch'ien's Residence

Open daily Monday to Friday from 9 a.m. to 4 p.m. (except national holidays). Visitors limited to 50 per day, 10 per visit. Children under the age of 12 not permitted. To schedule a visit, please contact the NPM Exhibition Department by phone and reconfirm by fax. Contact numbers: Tel: (886-2) 2881-2021 ex. 298, 683
Fax: (886-2) 2881-4138

Environs

San Hsi T'ang Tea Room

The San Hsi T'ang tea room, located in the central pavilion on the fourth floor of the main exhibition building, offers a selection of Chinese teas, pastries, and other snacks. The name San Hsi T'ang, which translates into English as "Hall of the Three Rarities," derives from the name of a study in the Forbidden City established by the Ch'ing emperor Ch'ien-lung. This room housed three of his most prized possessions, or the "three rarities": Wang Hsi-chih's *Clearing After Snowfall*, Wang Hsien-chih's *Chung-ch'iu t'ieh*, and Wang Hsun's *Po-yüan t'ieh*. These three works of calligraphy are among the most important and cherished works in the history of Chinese art.

The tearoom contains a reconstruction of Ch'ien-lung's study that offers a glimpse into the palace lifestyle of the Ch'ing emperors. The display also includes three famous works by Wang Hsi-chih: *Clearing After Snowfall*; *Three Passages: P'ing-an, Ho-ju, and Feng-chu*; and *The Distant Official*.

Chih-te Garden

If one were to characterize the Chih-shan garden as the imperial garden of the National Palace Museum, then the Chih-te garden would be its backyard. Occupying nearly a hectare of land, the garden is located approximately 100 meters down the driveway leading away from the Museum.

Upon entering through the garden's moon-shaped gate, the path splits in two directions. To the left, the winding walkway is divided into upper and lower sections. The lower section is covered by a canopy of foliage through which one can enjoy the murmurs of the adjacent stream. To the right, the path runs through a dark forested area between the stream and rising hillside. Moving further into the garden, one encounters its centerpiece—a large pond bedecked with a variety of lotus blossoms, the seasonal transformations of which present a moving tableau for all who cast their gaze upon the pond. After crossing a long, meandering bridge, one may ascend to a platform beside the garden's Cloud Gazing Pavilion, lean upon the rail, and take a last, long lingering view of the emerald scenery. Poised between heaven and earth, the leisurely atmosphere of the garden leaves its mark on all who venture here.

Chih-shan Garden

The entrance to the Chih-shan Garden is located off Chih-shan Road, to the right of the Museum's main entry concourse. Completed in 1985, this classical Chinese garden occupies over two hectares of land, and is filled with meandering walkways, pools, and pavilions. Upon entering the garden, one first encounters the Brush Washing Pool, an allusion to the famous calligrapher Chang Chih of the Eastern Han dynasty, who always wrote beside a pool of water in which he later washed his brushes. It is said that Chang was so prolific that his ink eventually turned the water black, giving the pool its distinctive name.

Moving further into the garden, one discovers two more pools. On the left is the Dragon Pool, from which a mythical Chinese creature known as a "Flood Dragon" emerges, spurting water and bringing good fortune. To the right is the second pool, overlooked by the Pavilion of the Emerald Bridge and Western Waters, a reference to a verse by the Southern Sung poet Wu Chu. It reads, "Overarched by hanging willow, emerald water streams below the bridge. The gentleman's house lies west, north beyond the bridge." A winding bridge with six bends spans the pool, connecting the pavilion and the opposite bank.

In the rear of the garden stands the Wind in Pines Pavilion. With the gray tiles of its saddleback roof and curving eaves, set against its natural spruce wood pillars, the entire structure exudes a simple and unadorned elegance. On the ground floor stands a stone tablet inscribed with the poem *Wind in Pines*, written in seven-character regulated verse by the Sung dynasty literatus Huang T'ing-chien.

The original edition of this work is part of the Museum's collection. By following the path that wraps around the building, one can ascend to the second floor and discover a zither, incense burner, and collection of poetry by the T'ang poet Tu Fu. Behind the table where these items are placed stands a six-sectioned screen inscribed with Mi Fu's famous work, *On Szechwan Silk*.

Beyond the Wind in Pines Pavilion stands a statue of Wang Hsi-chih exchanging a piece of his calligraphy for a caged goose. The image refers to the famous Chin dynasty calligrapher's fondness and compassion for geese. Moving further along the path, one can see the eight-cornered Orchid Pavilion with a Han dynasty style 'red sparrow' lantern resting on top, and a table with several classical Chinese drum-shaped stools inside. To the right of the pavilion stands a stele inscribed with a copy of Wang Hsi-chih's most famous work, the *Orchid Pavilion Preface*, taken from a rubbing in the collection of the Museum.

Continuing further to the right, one nears the garden's exit. Looking back across the pools and pavilions, one can almost imagine the teacups of Wang's *Orchid Pavilion Preface*, drifting on the languid water. Before departing, visitors may also stop briefly to have a look at the lovely birds in the aviary beside the exit. Together, the many features of the Chih-shan Garden fulfill our search for the aesthetic spirit of the traditional Chinese garden, and help us understand the importance of such an idyllic environment for traditional Chinese artists.

Residence of Chang Dai-ch'ien

From the entrance to the National Palace Museum, a short, ten-minute stroll up Chih-shan Road brings one to the Abode of Maya, the former residence of the famous painter Chang Dai-ch'ien (1899-1983), nestled in the heart of the community of Wai-shuang-hsi.

Chang's training in the art of brushwork began early in life, first under the auspices of his family, and later in the company of various masters. As a young man, he also spent over three years in the deserts of Kansu, studying and copying the mural painting in the caves of Tun-huang. Chang spent years laboriously studying the techniques of former masters, absorbing the stylistic essence of artists spanning the history of Chinese painting. He painted both small and monumental works, mastered the three classical subjects of Chinese painting—landscape, bird-and-flower, and figure painting—and perfected the techniques of meticulous, boneless, and plain line (*pai-miao*) brushwork. Chang also spent many years living abroad, where he obtained an international reputation and had the opportunity to visit famous scenic sites around the world. In later years, he developed his own unique painting style characterized by a sense of power and momentum, and the use of heavy, wet color. In these late works, he left a distinctive and indelible mark on the world of painting.

Constructed in 1976, Chang's residence occupies 1911 sq. meters of land. The rooms of the house are arranged in a square pattern that encloses a central

courtyard. The name Abode of Maya stems from a play on words founded on the phonetic similarity between the name Dai-chien and a religious reference to the "boundless universes" in the womb of Maya, the mother of Sakyamuni Buddha. One hundred days after Chang's passing, his heirs donated the residence to the National Palace Museum, and it was established as a memorial to his life and work.

Just inside the main gate is a small parking area that houses a large Lincoln automobile, Chang Dai-ch'ien personal vehicle. On the wall to the

right is an example of Chang's free and unrestrained hand. Winding into the inner courtyard, one discovers a garden featuring a pair of stone lions, a cascading coy pond, and an exquisite selection of flowering tea plants. Moving back into the

house, one finds a photo of Chang taken together with Pablo Picasso in 1956, an occasion when the two men met to discuss art and aesthetics. In the next room sits a life-size wax model of Chang, poised in the act of laying brush to paper. Beside him squats a gibbon, its attention focused on the artist and his work. Chang had a particular affinity for apes, as evidenced by the monkey enclosure constructed on the second floor of the house. It was said that he was a black gibbon in a former life, and he often signed his works with an archaic version of the character meaning 'gibbon' or 'ape', so that his signature read, quite literally, "Chang the Gibbon." Chang's studio also contains a list of the many famous works and artifacts that he donated to the National Palace Museum, a testament of both his desire to share beauty with the public and his lofty patriotism.

The second floor contains a small painting studio, mounting room, and bedroom. The sparsely furnished studio contains a wall clock, its hands fixed at 8:15 a.m., the time of Chang Dai-ch'ien's death. Behind the house a path winds through a luxuriant and expansive garden, its head overlooked by a willow. Set amidst the greenery is a large stone inscribed with the characters *mei ch'iu* (plum hill), that marks Chang's final resting spot. The rear portion of the garden is dominated by Ch'ang diverse collection of bonsai trees, which the artist lovingly searched out and gathered over the years. Within this area rest the I-ran and Fen-han pavilions, where one can rest and take in the surrounding beauty. The garden also contains a Barbeque Pavilion, where Chang used to hold Mongolian barbeques. Chang Hsüeh-liang donated the grill in the pavilion.

Chang Dai-ch'ien's residence reflects the spirit of a classical Chinese home. Furnished in a spare and elegant manner, it embodies the lyrical quality of Chinese painting and expresses the mood and manner of the traditional Chinese literati.

International Exhibitions

Over the course of the past ten years, the National Palace Museum has worked to build relationships with international museums, and expand the horizons of local audiences by hosting visiting exhibitions of artwork and cultural artifacts from overseas collections. These events have included exhibitions of works by Monet, Picasso, and Dali, treasures from the Louvre, archeological relics from San-hsing-tui, French painting, treasures from the Han dynasty, and artifacts from the cultures of the Eurasian steppes. These international exhibitions are held on the ground floor of the Library Building.

Mysteries of San-hsing-tui

De Poussin à Cézanne
從普桑到塞尚
法國繪畫三百年
多媒體導覽光碟

300 ANS DE PEINTURE FRANÇAISE

從普桑、華鐸、大衛、德拉克洛瓦到米勒、庫爾培、馬內、
雷諾瓦、莫內,至梵谷、高更、塞尚等等藝術大師筆下揮灑出的980幅巨作,
呈現法國繪畫三百年的發展軌跡!

精華導覽 蔣勳教授主講

魔幻·達利
Salvador Dalí 蔣勳 著

Downtown

Chih-sha

Tzu-ch'iang Tunnel

Library Building

Adminstration Bu

Wai-shuang-hsi

Chih-s

Shung Ye Museum of Formosan Aborigines

Transportation

MRT

Take the Tamsui Line to Shihlin Station, and transfer to bus number 304, 255, Red 30, or minibus number 18 or 19.

Bus

Take bus number 213, 304, 255, Red 30, or minibus number 18 or 19.

The Red 30 bus continues all the way up the Museum's driveway, stopping outside the Modern Art gallery (in front of the Hou-lo Garden).

Auto

If traveling by private automobile on the expressway, get off at the Pinchiang

-yin shan

Yang-ming shan

n

Museum Restaurant

Main Exhibition Building

den

interchange, drive through Tachih and take the Tzuchiang Tunnel to Museum Road. Turn right at Chih-shan Road to reach the Museum.

Taxi

The Information Desk, located just inside the entrance to the Main Exhibition Building, offers a free taxi call service.

Non-Chinese speaking visitors should provide the driver with the name of their destination written in Chinese. The Museum Information Desk is happy to provide assistance with this matter.

Index of Taipei Museums

■ National Palace Museum
Add: 221 Chih-shan Rd., Sec. 2, Wai-shuang-hsi, Taipei 111
Web: http://www.npm.gov.tw
Tel: (886-2) 2881-2021
Hours: Open daily 9 a.m to 5 p.m.

■ National Museum of History
Add: 49 Nan-hai Rd., Chungcheng, Taipei 100
Web: http://www.nmh.gov.tw/museum/index.html
Tel: (886-2) 2361-0270
Hours: 10 a.m. to 6 p.m.
Closed: Mondays, New Year's Eve, Chinese New Year

■ Taiwan Museum
Add: 2 Hsian-yang Rd., Chungcheng, Taipei 100
Web: http://www.tpm.gov.tw
Tel: (886-2) 2382-2699
Hours: 10 a.m. to 5 p.m.
Closed: Mondays, New Year's Eve, Chinese New Year, first week of December

■ National Taiwan Arts Education Institute
Add: 47 Nan-hai Rd., Chungcheng, Taipei 100
Web: http://www.nmh.gov.tw/art/index.html
Tel: (886-2) 2311-0574
Hours: Open daily 9 a.m. to 5 p.m.

■ National Dr. Sun Yat-sen Memorial Hall
Add: 505, Jen-ai Rd., Sec. 4, Hsinyi, Taipei 110
Web: http://www.yatsen.gov.tw
Tel: (886-2) 2758-8008
Hours: 9 a.m. to 5 p.m.
Closed: New Year's Eve, Chinese New Year

■ Chiang Kai-Shek Memorial Hall
Add: 21 Chung-shan S. Rd., Chungcheng, Taipei 100
Web: http://www.cksmh.gov.tw
Tel: (886-2) 2343-1100~3
Hours: 9 a.m. to 5 p.m.
Closed: June 15, December15, New Year's Eve, Chinese New Year, Dragon Boat
          Festival, Mid-Autumn Festival

■National Taiwan Science Education Centre
Add: 189, Shih-shang. Rd., Shihlin, Taipei 111
Web: http://www.ntsec.gov.tw
Tel: (886-2) 6610-1234
Hours: 9 a.m. to 5 p.m.
Closed: Mondays

■Taipei Fine Arts Museum
Add: 181, Chung-shan N. Rd., Sec. 3, Chungshan, Taipei 104
Web: http://www.tfam.gov.tw
Tel: (886-2) 2595-7656
Hours: 10 a.m. to 6 p.m.
Closed: Mondays

■Taipei Astronomical Museum
Add: 363 Kee-ho Rd., Shihlin, Taipei 111
Web: http://www.tam.gov.tw
Tel: (886-2) 2831-4551
Hours: 9 a.m. to 9 p.m.
Closed: Mondays, days following national holidays

■Taipei Children's Museum of Transportation & Communication
Add: 2, Ting-juo Rd., Sec. 3, Chungcheng, Taipei 100
Web: http://www.kidspark.com.tw
Tel: (886-2) 2369-0001
Hours: 9 a.m. to 5:30 p.m.
Closed: New Year's Eve, Chinese New Year

■228 Memorial Museum
Add: 3 Kaidagelan Blvd., Chungcheng, Taipei 100
Web: http://www.t228.gov.tw
Tel: (886-2) 2389-7228
Hours: 10 a.m. to 5 p.m. (Free admission on Wednesdays)
Closed: Mondays

■Peitou Hotspring Museum
Add: 2 Chung-shan Rd., Peitou, Taipei 112
Tel: (886-2) 2893-9981～5
Hours: 9 a.m. to 5 p.m.
Closed: Mondays, national holidays

■ Postal Museum
Add: 45, Chung-ching S. Rd., Sec. 2, Chungcheng, Taipei 100
Web: http://www.post.gov.tw
Tel: (886-2) 2394-5185~7
Hours: 9 a.m. to 5 p.m.
Closed: Mondays, days following national holidays, Chinese New Year,
          Dragon Boat Festival, Mid-Autumn Festival

■ Mongolian and Tibetan Affairs Commission
Add: 3, Lane 8, Ching-tian St., Taan, Taipei 106
Web: http://www.mtac.gov.tw
Tel: (886-2) 2351-4280
Hours: 9 a.m. to 5 p.m.
Closed: Regular and national holidays

■ Information Science and Technology Exhibition Center
Add: 108, He-ping E. Rd., Sec. 2, Taan, Taipei 106
Web: http://www.istec.iii.org.tw
Tel: (886-2) 2737-7032
Hours: 9 a.m. to 5 p.m.
Closed: Mondays, New Year's Eve, Chinese New Year

■ Taipei Water Department
Add: 1 Ssu-yuan St., Chungcheng, Taipei 100
Web: http://www.twd.gov.tw/chinese/04sales/d_03.htm
Tel: (886-2) 8369-5145
Hours: 9 a.m. to 5 p.m.
Closed: Mondays

■ Museum of the Institute of Ethnology, Academia Sinica
Add: 128 Yen-chiu-yuan Rd., Sec. 2, Nankang, Taipei 115
Web: http://www.sinica.edu.tw/ioe/tool/museum
Tel: (886-2) 2652-3308
Hours: 9 a.m to 12 p.m., 1:30 p.m. to 5 p.m.
Closed: Sundays and national holidays

■ Museum of the Institute of History and Philology, Academia Sinica
Add: 130 Yen-chiu-yuan Rd., Sec. 2, Nankang, Taipei 115
Web: http://museum.sinica.edu.tw
Tel: (886-2) 2652-3180
Hours: Wednesdays and Saturdays 9:30 a.m. to 4:30 p.m.

■Chang Foundation

Add: 63, Jen-ai Rd., Sec. 2, Chungcheng, Taipei 100

Web: http://www.changfound.org.tw

Tel: (886-2) 2356-9575

Hours: 10:30 a.m. to 4:30 p.m.

Closed: Mondays, Chinese New Year, National Tomb-Sweeping Day (April 5)

■The Taipei Municipal Cheng-kung Senior High School Insect Museum

Add: 71, Chi-nan Rd., Sec. 1, Chungcheng, Taipei 100

Web: http://library.cksh.tp.edu.tw

Tel: (886-2) 2396-1298 #13

Hours: 9 a.m. to 11:30 a.m., 2 p m. to 4:00 p.m.

   (half days during winter and summer vacations)

Closed: Regular and national holidays

■Taiwan Forestry Exhibition Hall

Add: 60, Nan-hai Rd., Chungcheng, Taipei 100

Web: http://www.tfri.gov.tw

Tel: (886-2) 2303-9978 #3852

Hours: 8:30 a.m. to 11:30 a.m., 1:30 p.m. 4:30 p.m.

Closed: Saturdays, Chinese New Year, National Tomb-Sweeping Day (April 5),

   Dragon Boat Festival, Mid-Autumn Festival

■Ho Gallery of Calligraphic Arts Foundation

Add: B1, 222, Chin-shan S. Rd., Sec. 2, Taan, Taipei 106

Web: http://chinesecalligraphy.org.tw

Tel: (886-2) 2393-9899

Hours: 10 a.m. to 5 p.m.

Closed: Mondays

■Taipei Botanic Garden

Add: 53 Nan-hai Rd., Chungcheng, Taipei 100 (Taiwan Forestry Research Institute)

Web: http://www.tfri.gov.tw

Tel: (886-2) 2303-9978

Hours: Open daily 4 a.m. to 10 p.m.

   (8:30 a.m. to 4:30 p.m. for the area around the greenhouse)

Yuyu Yang Museum

Add: 31, Chung-ching S. Rd., Sec. 2, Chungcheng, Taipei 100
Web: http://yuyuyang.e-lib.nctu.edu.tw
Tel: (886-2) 2396-1966
Hours: Monday to Saturday 11 a.m. to 5 p.m.
Closed: Sundays

Taipei Zoo

Add: 30, Hsin-kuang Rd., Sec. 2, Wenshan, Taipei 116
Web: http://www.zoo.gov.tw
Tel: (886-2) 2938-2300~9
Hours: 8:30 a.m. to 5 p.m. for Zoo ; 9 a.m. to 4:30 p.m. for Education Center
Closed: New Year's Eve

NTU Anthropology Exhibiton Room

Add: 1, Roosevelt Rd., Sec. 4, Taan, Taipei 106
Web: http://ccsun57.cc.ntu.edu.tw~anthro/english/e_index..html
Tel: (886-2) 2363-0231#2299
Hours: Friday 10 a.m. to 12 p.m., NTU's anniversary
Closed: Winter and summer vacations

Agricultural Exhibition Hall

Add: 1, Roosevelt Rd., Sec. 4, Taan, Taipei 106
Web: http://www-ms.cc.ntu.edu.tw/~hall
Tel: (886-2) 2362-7788
Hours: Monday to Friday 9 a.m. to 4:50 p.m.
Closed: Regular holidays (expect for special exhibitions)

Taipei Tea Promotion Center for Tie Kuanyin Tea and Pachung Tea

Add: 8-2, Lane 40, Chih-nan Rd., Sec. 3, Wenshan, Taipei 116
Web: http://www.liukung.org.tw
Tel: (886-2) 2234-0568
Hours: 9 a.m. to 5 p.m. (10 a.m. to 11 a.m., 2 p.m. to 3 p.m. for Soil Conservation Room)
Closed: Mondays

Lee Shih Chiao Art Museum

Add: 3 Fl., 218-7, Chung-hsiao E. Rd., Sec. 4, Taan, Taipei 106
Tel: (886-2) 2741-5638~9
Hours: Sundays 2 p.m. to 5 p.m. (group tours provided on other days by appointment)
Closed: Last Sunday of each month

■Fo Kuan Yuan Art Gallery (Taipei Gallery)

Add: 10 Fl.-1, 327, Sung-lung Rd., Hsinyi, Taipei 110
Web: http://www.fgs.org.tw/fgyan/art/ART-A.htm
Tel: (886-2) 2760-0222
Hours: 10 a.m. to 9 p.m.
Closed: New Year's Eve

■Wei Chin-Yuan Musical Instruments Museum

Add: 9-1, Alley 17, Lane 181, Pa-te Rd., Sec. 4, Sungshan, Taipei 105
Web: http://www.wmim.idv.tw
Tel: (886-2) 2742-3333
Hours: Saturdays and Sundays 10 a.m. to 6 p.m.

■Anti-Disaster Technology and Educational Training Museum

Add: 376, Cheng-kung Rd., Sec. 2, Neihu, Taipei 114
Web: http://www.tfd.gov.tw
Tel: (886-2) 2791-9786
Hours: 9 a.m. to 12 a.m., 2 p.m. to 5 p.m.
Closed: Mondays, New Year's Eve, Chinese New Year

■The Rock Hounds Museum

Add: 1, Alley 17, Lane 121, Cheng-fu Rd., Nankang, Taipei 115
Web: http://www.apple.com.tw/rockcomp
Tel: (886-2) 2651-8407
Hours: 9 a.m. to 5 p.m. (please call in advance to arrange a visit)

■Customs Museum

Add: 13 Ta-cheng St., Tatung, Taipei 103
Web: http://www.dogc.gov.tw
Tel: (886-2) 2550-5500# 2212～6
Hours: Saturdays and Sundays from 10 a.m. to 5 p.m.

■Museum of Contemporary Art, Taipei

Add: 39 Chang-an W. Rd., Tatung, Taipei 103
Web: http://www.mocataipai.org.tw
Tel: (886-2) 2552-3720
Hours: 10 a.m. to 6 p.m.
Closed: Mondays

■ TTT Tuppet Center
Add: 66 Ming-le St., Tatung, Taipei 103
Web: http://www.taiuan.org.tw
Tel: (886-2) 2552-8344
Hours: 10 a.m. to 5:30 p.m.
Closed: Mondays, Sundays, national holidays

■ SuHo Memorial Paper Museum
Add: 68, Chang-an E. Rd., Sec. 2, Chungshan, Taipei 104
Web: http://www.shopaper.org.tw
Tel: (886-2) 2507-5539
Hours: 9:30 a.m. to 4:30 p.m. (please call in advance to arrange a visit)
Closed: Sundays, Founding Day of the Republic of China (January 1), Chinese New
          Year, National Tomb-sweeping Day (April 5), Dragon Boat Festival, Mid-Autumn
          Festival

■ Miniatures Museum of Taiwan
Add: B1, 96, Chien-kuo N. Rd., Sec.1, Chungshan, Taipei 104
Web: http://www.mmot.com.tw
Tel: (886-2) 2515-0583
Hours: 10 a.m. to 6 p.m.
Closed: Mondays

■ Taipei Children's Recreation Center
Add: 66, Chung-shan N. Rd., Sec. 3, Chungshan, Taipei 104
Web: http://www.tmcrc.gov.tw
Tel: (886-2) 2593-2211# 231, 209
Hours: 9 a.m. to 5 p.m.
Closed: Mondays, New Year's Eve, morning of Chinese New Year

■ Lin An-tai Ancestral Home
Add: 5 Pin-chiang St., Chungshan, Taipei 104
Web: http://www.tbroc.gov.tw
Tel: (886-2) 2598-1572
Hours: 9 a.m. to 5 p.m.
Closed: Mondays

■ Shin Chien University Costume Museum
Add: 70 Ta-chih St., Chungshan, Taipei 104
Web: http://www.usc.edu.tw/college/clothes/museum/index.htm
Tel: (886-2) 2537-1111, 2533-8151 #7063
Hours: 9 a.m. to 5 p.m.
Closed: Saturdays, Sundays, winter and summer vacation

■Taipei Sea World
Add: 128 Chi-ho Rd., Shihlin, Taipei 111
Web: http://www.fins.com.tw
Tel: (886-2) 2880-3636
Hours: 9 a.m. to 10 p.m.
Closed: New Year's Eve

■Shung Ye Museum of Formosan Aborigines
Add: 282 Chih-shan Rd., Sec. 2, Shihlin, Taipei 111
Web: http://www.museum.org.tw
Tel: (886-2) 2841-2611
Hours: 9 a.m. to 5 p.m.
Closed: Mondays, January 20 to February 20

■Taiwan Folk Arts Museum
Add: 32 You-ya Rd., Peitou, Taipe 112
Tel: (886-2) 2891 2318, 2891-8954
Hours: 10 a.m.to 7 p.m.
Closed: Mondays

■Grand Crystal Museum
Add: 16, Lane 515, Chung-yang N. Rd., Sec. 4, Peitou, Taipei 112
Web: http://www.tittot.com
Tel: (886-2) 2895-8861
Hours: 9 a.m. to 5 p.m.
Closed: Mondays

■TNUA Kuandu Museum of Art
Add: 1 Hsuen-yuen Rd., Peitou, Taipei 112
Web: http://www.nia.edu.tw
Tel: (886-2) 2896-1000 #3335
Hours: 10 a.m.to 5 p.m.
Closed: Mondays

■Hong-Gah Museum
Add: 5 Fl., 260 Ta-yeh Rd., Peitou, Taipei 112
Web: http://www.hong-gah.org.tw
Tel: (886-2) 2894-2272
Hours: 10:30 a.m. to 5:30 p.m.
Closed: Mondays

Pin Lin Tea Museum
Add: 19-1 Shueisungchilkeng, Pinglin Township, Taipe 232
Web: http://www.pingling.tpc.gov.tw/teahouse/organ.htm
Tel: (886-2) 2665-6035
Hours: Regular days 9 a.m. to 5 p.m., holidays 9 a.m. to 6 p.m.
Closed: Mondays

Taipei Country Yingko Ceramics Museum
Add: 200 Wenhua Rd., Yingge Township, Taipei 239
Web: http://www.ceramics.tpc.gov.tw
Tel: (886-2) 8677-2727
Hours: Tuesday to Friday 9:30 a.m. to 5 p.m., weekends 9:30 a.m. to 6 p.m.
Closed: Mondays

Shi-San Hang Museum of Archaeology
Add: 200 Bowuguan Rd., Bali Township, Taipei 249
Web: http://www.sshm.gov.tw
Tel: (886-2) 2619-1313
Hours: Tuesday to Friday 9:30 a.m. to 5 p.m., Saturday until 8 p.m., Sunday unti 6 p.m.
Closed: Mondays

Tamkang University Maritime Museum
Add: 151 Yingjuan Rd., Danshuei Township, Taipei 251
Web: http://lib.tku.edu.tw/museum/index.htm
Tel: (886-2) 2623-8343
Hours: 9 a.m. to 4 p.m.
Closed: Mondays, days after national holidays, Dragon Boat Festival, Mid-Autumn
        Festival, New Year Eve, winter vacation

Juming Museum
Add: 2 She-shi-hu, Chin-shan Township, Taipei 208
Web: http://www.juming.org.tw
Tel: (886-2) 2498-9940
Hours: 10 a.m. to 6 p.m. May to October, 10 a.m. to 5 p.m. November to April
Closed: Mondays, days after national holidays, New Year's Eve

Dausheng China Weapons Museum
Add: 72-1, Beitoutz, Danshuei Township, Taipei 251
Tel: (886-2) 2623-8417
Hours: Please call in advance to arrange a visit

■ Taiwan Power Company North Vistors Center
Add: 60 Badou Rd., Wanli Township, Taipei 207
Tel: (886-2) 2498-5112-3
Hours: 8:20 a.m. to 4:20 p.m.
Closed: Mondays, days after national holidays, New Year's Eve, Chinese New Year

■ Litienlu Puppet Museum
Add: 26 Jhibo Rd., Sanjr Township, Taipei 252
Tel: (886-2) 2636-4715, 2636-7330
Hours: Saturday and Sunday from 9 a.m. to 5 p.m. (other days by appointment only)

■ Chuenhe Children's Toys Museum
Add. 150-1, Daliau Rd., Rueifang Township, Taipei 224
Tel: (886-2) 2462-5331
Hours: Regular days 10 a.m. to 5 p.m., Friday, Saturday 9 a.m. to 5 p.m.

■ Jiou Fen Goldmine Museum
Add: 66, Lane Shrbei, Shuchi Rd., Rueifang Township, Taipei 224
Tel: (886-2) 2496 6379
Hours: 8 a.m. to 6 p.m. (Please call in advance to arrange a visit)

■ Kite Museum
Add: 20, Lane Kenguei, Shuchi Rd., Rueifang Township, Taipei 224
Tel: (886-2) 2496-7709
Hours: 9 a.m. to 7 p.m.

■ Chin Die Gu Insects Ecosystem Farm
Add: 18 Alley 499, Lane 499, Siwan Rd., Sijhih City, Taipei 221
Tel: (886-2) 2646-4845
Hours: Regular holidays 9 a.m. to 5 p.m. (other days by appointment only)

■ Cheng Feng Shian Millimeter Sculpture Gallery
Add: 17, Lane 207, Ankang Rd., Sec.1, Shindian City, Taipei 231
Tel: (886-2) 2212-5794
Hours: Sunday 10 a.m. to 5 p.m.

■HuaFan Culture Gallery
Add: 1 Hua Fan Rd., Shriding Township, Taipei 223
Web: http://www.hfu.edu.tw/~gfc
Tel: (886-2) 2663-2102 #3201, 3202
Hours: 8 a.m. to 4:30 p.m.
Closed: Chinese New Year

■Taipei Nostalgic Museum
Add: 164 Jianguo Rd., Shindian City, Taipei 231
Web: http://home.kimo.com.tw/wangdavidi
Tel: (886-2) 2913-0860
Hours: 9 a.m. to 8 p.m. (Please call in advance to arrange a visit)

■Wulai Aborigines Exhibit Room
Add: 5 Laka Rd., Wulai Township, Taipei 223
Web: wujh.tpc.edu.tw/index/menu4/menu4-5.htm
Tel: (886-2) 2661-6482
Hours: Please call in advance to arrange a visit

■Museum of World Religions
Add: 7 Fl., 236, Jungshan Rd., Sec. 1, Yunghe City, Taipei 234
Web: http://www.mwr.org.tw
Tel: (886-2) 8231-6666
Hours: Regular days 10 a.m. to 6 p.m.; Fridays, Saturdays, and national holidays 10 a.m.
        to 10 p.m.
Hours: Mondays, days after national holidays, New Year's Eve, Chinese New Year

■Yang San Lang Arts Museum
Add: 7 Boai St., Yunghe City, Taipei 234
Tel: (886-2) 2928-7692, 2921-2960
Hours: Sunday 10 a.m. to 4 p.m. (group tours provided on other days for over 20 persons
        by appointment)

■Fujen Cathloic University Textiles and Clothing Teaching
Add: 510 Jungjeng Rd., Shinjuang City, Taipei 242
Tel: (886-2) 2903-1111 #3647
Hours: 8 a.m. to 4:30 p.m. (Please call in advance to arrange a visit)

■Li Mei-shu Professor Memorial Cultural Relicts Gallery
Add: 6 Fl., 119 Minsheng St., Sanshia Township, Taipei 237
Tel: (886-2) 2673-8399
Hours: Sunday 11 a.m. to 5 p.m. (Please call in advance to arrange a visit)

■Hsiao Hsi Yuan Play Doll Presentation Gallery
Add: 489 Shinjuang Rd., Shinjuang City, Taipei 242
Tel: (886-2) 2203-7916
Hours: 2 p.m. to 10 p.m.
Closed: Saturdays and Sundays

■Li Mei-shu Memorial Gallery
Add: 10, Lane 43, Junghua Rd., Sanshia Township, Taipei 237
Web: http://www.limeishu.org
Tel: (886-2) 2673-2333
Hours: Regular and national holidays 10 a.m. to 5 p.m. (group tours provided on other
        days by appointment)

■The Forbidden City Curio Cultural Relics House
Add: 30-1 Desheng St., Lujon City, Taipoi 247
Web: http://www.twist.com.tw/95
Tel: (886-2) 8282-7504 (please call 0918-084 007 to arrange a visit)
Hours: Saturdays and Sundays 2:30 p.m. to 5 p.m.

acoustiguide

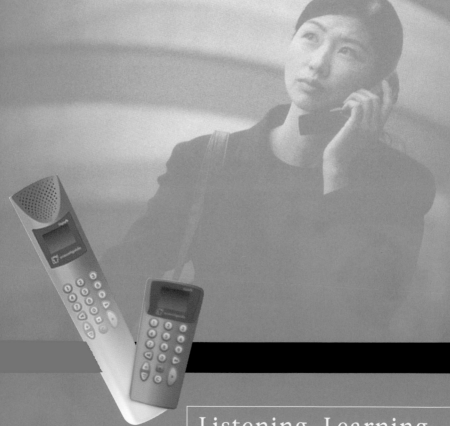

Listening=Learning

With more
than **40** years
of experience

...in the studio and in the field, Acoustiguide is your
partner in audio interpretation from concept to closing time.

Acoustiguide Worldwide

More than 40 years ago, Acoustiguide invented the audio tour, and the company has
remained at the leading edge of creativity and technology ever since. Acoustiguide
provides audio programs for museums, heritage and historic sites, tourism attractions,
zoos, aquariums, and corporate clients in 22 countries around the world and in nearly
20 languages, including English, French, German, Italian, Spanish, Chinese,
Japanese, Dutch, Polish, Russian, Tibetan, and Maori. Acoustiguide offers complete
creative and production services, the most advanced audio technology and
comprehensive on-site management.

Acoustiguide in Taiwan

Established in 1995, with its headquarter in USA, Acoustiguide Asia Ltd., Taiwan
Branch is the nation's leading company in providing high quality audio tours to
numerous museums, galleries, heritage sites, and science centers, including the
National Palace Museum, Taipei Fine Arts Museum, National History Museum, Taiwan
Museum of Art, Museum of Contemporary Arts, National Museum of Prehistory,
National Science and Technology Museum, National Museum of Natural Sciences, and
National Center of Traditional Arts. We aim to offer visitors new and interesting insights
into cultural attractions. Over the last eight years, we have produced audio programs
in Mandarin, English, Japanese, Taiwanese, and Hakka.

No one has produced more audio tours or engaged more visitors than Acoustiguide

Acoustiguide Asia Ltd., Taiwan Branch
10/F, 143, Nan-ching East Rd., Sec. 4, Taipei 105, Taiwan R.O.C
Tel: (886-2) 2713-5355 Fax: (886-2) 2717-5403 E-mail: info@acoustiguide.com.tw
http://www. acoustiguide.com

Chinese Chronology

Neolithic period
Mythical sovereigns: Shen-nung, Huang-ti, Yao, Shun
Hsia 2207-1766 B.C.

Shang 1765-1122 B.C.

Western Chou 1122-771 B.C.

Eastern Chou 770-256 B.C.
Spring and Autumn period 722-482 B.C.
Warring States period 453-221 B.C.

Ch'in
221-206 B.C.

Western Han
206B.C.-A.D. 9

Hsin/Wang Mang Interregnum
9-25

Eastern Han
25-220

Three Kingdoms
220-265

Western Chin
265-316

Eastern Chin
317-420

North and South Dynasties *420-589*
Sui *581-618*
T'ang *618-907*
Five Dynasties *907-960*
Northern Sung *960 1127*
Southern Sung *1127-1279*
Yüan *1271-1368*
Ming *1368-1644*
Ch'ing *1644-1911*
Republic of China *1912-*

Based on Jacques Gernet, *A History of Chinese Civilization*,
2ⁿᵈed., trans. J. R. Foster and Charles Hartman (Cambridge: Cambridge University Press, 1996)
* All dates prior to 842 B.C. are tentative.

National Palace Museum Guidebook

Publisher ■ Lin Chiu-fang

Editorial Commissioners ■

Wang Yo-ting, Liu Cheng-yun, Chang Kuang-yuen,

Hu Sai-lan, Lee Saalih, Teng Shu-ping, Chi Jo-hsin

Production ■ Acoustiguide Asia Ltd., Taiwan Branch

General Editor ■ Lin Chiu-fang

Editorial Consultant ■ Wang Hui-min

Editors in Chief ■ Chen Jie-jin, Hsu Chun-hsien

Editor ■ Aquarius Culture & Art Center

Lead Translator ■ Jeffrey Moser

Translators ■ Albert Wu, Phillip Wu, Erika Nishizato

Art Director ■ Wu Chun-hui

Designer ■ Wuprint Creative Co. Ltd.

Art Editor ■ Lin Cheng-ru

Illustrator ■ Chen Yung-mo (Chinese morochrome)

Marketing Coordinators & Administrators ■

Fu Hui-hui, Chuang Ya-shan

Proof-readers ■ Fu Hui-hui, Chuang Ya-shan

Photographs Provided by ■ National Palace Museum

Audio Tour ■ Acoustiguide Asia Ltd., Taiwan Branch

Printer ■ Suhai Design And Production

···

Acoustiguide Asia Ltd., Taiwan Branch

10 Fl., 143, Nan-ching E. Rd., Sec.4, Sungshan,

Taipei, Taiwan 105, R.O.C.

Tel ■ 886-2-2713-5355 Fax ■ 886-2-2717-5403

E-mail ■ info@acoustiguide.com.tw

First published 2003, second impression 2005

ISBN 957-30527-4-1